Brighton Unemployed Centre
Families Project

Salt And Vinegar

SALT: NOUN
1) A white crystalline solid, chiefly sodium chloride, used to flavour and preserve food
2) An element that gives flavour or zest
3) Sharp lively wit

VINEGAR: NOUN
1) A dilute solution of acetic acid used to flavour and preserve food
2) Sourness of speech or mood; bad temper
3) Eagerness and enthusiasm; vim

Dedicated to the staff, trustees and volunteers at Brighton Unemployed Centre Families Project. You are an extraordinary team doing extraordinary things.

This place is like compost. I'm an outsider,
living on the margins, but here I can put down roots
Centre user

First published in 2008
by Waterloo Press (Hove)
126 Furze Croft
Furze Hill
Hove BN3 1PF

Printed in Palatino 11pt by
One Digital
54 Hollingdean Road
East Sussex BN2 4AA

Edited by Bridget Whelan © 2008
Cover illustration by Allison Clare and the BUCFP Art Group © 2008
Cover design and typesetting Alan Morrison © 2008

A CIP record for this book is available
from the British Library

ISBN 1-902731-33-6

Acknowledgements

Thank you to Awards for All, the lottery grant making scheme, and Brighton and Hove Council. The financial support of these two organisations made *Salt and Vinegar* possible.

It would have stayed an idea, however, without Lisa Marshall, the Centre's fundraiser, and Ellie Moulton, the Participation Worker responsible for the day-to-day running of the project. Things happen because of Ellie and Lisa, because they refuse to be overawed by problems. Others ask why: they ask why not.

Warms thanks also to Peter Sutcliffe, the Education Worker, for giving *Salt and Vinegar* a virtual reality on the web and for practical support in numerous ways throughout the course of the project.

A whole team of Centre volunteers stepped forward to make sure that everything happened when it was supposed to happen: they proofread, they typed, they organised. They also made difficult decisions about commas. Thank you to Richard Ince and Yvonne Luna. Thank you to Valérie de Schaller and Jenny Corbin. Thank you to Josie Darling who helped with this project and also the weekly creative writing classes. At the risk of sounding like the worst kind of cliché, not one voice was raised in the making of this anthology, not one temper frayed at the edges.

Special thanks has to go to Simon Jenner of Waterloo Press who has been involved from the very first, guiding us through the printing and publishing process. I'm not sure you can have your hand held over the phone but that was what it felt like.

The designer Alan Morrison is a poet in words and visual images. We are grateful for his patience and his understanding of what BUCFP is trying to achieve.

The support of David Lepper, Member of Parliament for Brighton Pavilion, was very important to *Salt and Vinegar*'s success and we are grateful for his interest. We would also like to express our appreciation to Alan Issler Principal Library Manager, Community and Development and staff at Jubilee Library for hosting the launch of *Salt and Vinegar* on World Book Day 2008.

Finally, thank you to all the writers whose work is published within these pages.

Introduction

Welcome to *Salt and Vinegar*, an anthology produced by Brighton Unemployed Centre Families Project, a community centre in the heart of the city. Much of what follows grew out of short, against-the-clock writing exercises in workshops and tutorials that ran throughout the summer and autumn of 2007. For some authors this was their first experience of expressing themselves in writing. For many it was the first time they had written about their own lives.

Financial support from Awards for All and Brighton and Hove Council made this book possible: the talent and courage of the contributors have transformed the original idea into a bitter sweet collection of writing that has the power to move.

The American sports journalist Red Smith once said that there's nothing to writing: "All you do is sit down at a typewriter and open a vein." There is an honesty in these pages that suggests it could almost be true and it is only when you see it on the page that you realise how rare a quality it is.

There were tears during workshops, and goosebump moments when a passage of writing was read aloud that cut clear to the heart of everything that matters. There was also laughter and gasps of recognition as we travelled back in time remembering how things used to be.

The result is strong, powerful, life writing; it's not always a comfortable read but it is always engaging. There is murder within these pages, raw and real, and the struggle to understand mental distress. There is loneliness and fear next to moments of sheer unadulterated pleasure: whether it is singing in Hove or working in San Francisco's gay leather industry. There are memories of school and teenage snogging sessions, first jobs and first loves, portraits of family life and the heartbreak of homes broken by death and divorce.

You will find here descriptions that get under the skin of memory. Visit Butlins of the 1950s in the vocabulary of a 1950s child and relive the agony of waiting for Butterscotch Angel Delight to set. Share too the adult agony of an unplanned pregnancy and come close to understanding the impossibility of making the right decision.

The title *Salt and Vinegar* hints at the challenges and contradictions that life can throw up, while also giving the anthology a distinctive seaside flavour. Much of the writing has made in Brighton embedded in the ink. Like the city, there are passages of extraordinary beauty and craftsmanship sitting cheek by jowl with neighbours that are a little rough around the edges, threatening to crumble under the weight of adjectives (the editing has been deliberately gentle). It reflects Brighton's cosmopolitan outlook too. Writing criss-crosses the globe from voodoo practices in Cuba and bird eating snakes in Australia to cruel poverty in rural Ireland.

We all have many identities, and Brighton is no exception: often called London by the Sea (although really it is more like Camden and Islington with a pebble beach), it is also referred to as Cool City, UK and the damp end of Wardour Street. However, we are perhaps most accurately defined as Blow-In City.

The authors of *Salt and Vinegar* have come from Calcutta and White hawk, South London and Switzerland, Hove and Alabama, Newhaven and Nottingham and when you glance through the biographies at the end of the book, it is clear that they have come to the Centre for different reasons: they can't be slotted into a one-size-fits-all pigeon hole. Perhaps the only quality they share is the need to be part of a community centre that respects those differences. One writer, with a nice home in the right part of town, has been coming to the Centre for years. There's poverty of emotion as well as poverty, she told me with tears in her eyes. This place helps with both kinds.

As Writer in Residence, in a small way I've become part of the ebb and flow of Centre life, and that has helped me to understand the important role it plays in so many people's lives. I have felt the quietness at the heart of the Centre that can't be destroyed by crying babies, squeals of laughter from the crèche, or the occasional thump of saucepans from the kitchen. I'm not sure how to describe it except to borrow my son's language. Safe is the highest word of praise from his lips and the Centre is safe. It is a place of safety.

Outside might be confusing, uncertain, a swamp of regulations; outside you might feel very small. In the Centre – where in its 26-year history there has never been a boss – everyone is the same size.

I don't want to give the impression of inactivity though. This is a busy, busy place. You can develop key vocational skills in the crèche (which is described as wonderful so often it seems to be part of its name), in the kitchen and the office. You can paint pictures that will be part of a Festival exhibition, wash clothes, furnish your home and eat well and cheaply.

I'm tempted to say the Centre also solves problems, and I know that the Welfare Advice Service does exactly that, but some of the writing in this anthology explores experiences where there can never be a solution. Yet the Centre can still help people to heal and grow stronger, to be the best they possibly can, no matter what life has thrown at them or taken away.

This is a very human place and this is a very human anthology.

Bridget Whelan
Writer in Residence

Contents

The Young Ones

'My best friend Fiona thought she was a camel. So I said I would be a carrot.'
Laila Raphael

We Are Family

'Madness entered my childhood home through the back door …' *Josephine*

Teenage Kicks

'So I went to Kevin and said…'let's go to Brighton beach and give sandwiches to the homeless...' *Ged Duncan*

It's Off To Work We Go

'I can't swim," he snapped back at me, while throwing one leg over the railing. He was now precariously poised over the edge...*Ty Galvin*

Home Sweet Home

'It is a Presbyterian chair, comfortable and high quality, like a nice piece of cheese...' *Josie Darling*

Ticket To Ride

'I saw my first boat. It glinted harshly in the wet light. It was as cold as iron and there were cattle on the lower deck...' *Joe Sheerin*

Photographs and Memories

'I let my mind wander into the past, where at least I have control over where I go…' *A.K.Andrew*

What a Wonderful World

'…we were encouraged to feel life come into our limbs and, as it came, to feel the connection with the earth itself…' *Pat Bowen*

Time To Say Goodbye

'The north wind blew cool as he gently closed his large brown orbs….'
Maggs Radcliffe

Stand By Me

'The Centre is part of my life...' *Richard Ince*

The Young Ones

Angel Delight
by Yvonne Luna

Angel Delight: would it set? Could we wait for it to set? Are you joking? OVERNIGHT? Eaten still liquidly. Not as good, no. BUT HOW WAIT? 20 minutes? What would we do while waiting? How do you fill the ache of an *Angel Delight* 20 minute wait? THE ACHE. Not so bad if it's strawberry, because that's not my favourite. We work out a plan: make several at the same time, then we can be distracted from the WAIT by making more, and eating raw virgin baby liquidly unripe *Angel Delight* to fill the ache while we wait for

THE BANANA

Tastes like heaven. Angel's Delight. Eaten by Angels – that's why they can fly, that's why they are tiny and magical: because this is what they eat – all day long! Breakfast, lunch and tea! This is the order:

　　1st Banana
　　2nd Butterscotch
　　3rd Chocolate
　　4th Strawberry

It has set into its moosy consistency. We let it linger two seconds on our tongue before we wolf the whole lot down. And mix yellow, pink and brown in our tummies.
　We keep going.
　Nobody is watching.
　We bought a whole boxful from cash and carry.
　We can do it.
　The whole box
　in a week.
　We are many.
　We are strong.
　We are IN LOVE
　We are singing with the angels.

It's good for us apparently; it's got milk in it…

No Time for Trains
by Ty Galvin

As I walked up the avenue to my house, I saw an open back truck coming towards me. It was stacked with furniture and I recognised immediately it was from our house. My darkest fears were realised. I was eight years old and as I left for school that morning my mother warned me that something terrible could happen to-day. The bailiffs were coming and if daddy could not find any money for them they would take our furniture and any goods they could sell. I clasped the straps of the school bag on my back, put my head down, kept walking and tried not to look as the slow moving load came towards me, it was only a hundred yards to our gate.

It was a well to do area and I could hear the friendly 'helloes' and 'don't worries' from some neighbours, and felt the sniggering and slagging from the snide ones, I finally reached our front gate and quickened my steps to the front door where my mother was waiting to take me inside. She closed the door and hugged me. The gruff voice of my father came from upstairs.

"Is that the boy? Don't be mollycoddling him and bring my medicine up".

He was sick in bed with pneumonia and injuries sustained in a car accident and had not been able to work for some time. There was no money coming in, commitments could not be met, hence the bailiffs.

In 1948 in Ireland the welfare state had not arrived, much less the compensation culture, so any help possible would have had to come from good intentioned charities. My Dad, a fiercely independent man – the youngest person on active service in the War of Independence – could not even contemplate charity. That was something for the poor, not for someone in his position. Our furniture had gone, the house was about to go and we didn't know where our next meal was coming from. We could not have been more skint.

For months preceding this, my mother tried to prepare me for the worsening situation; saying I had to be a man, I must not cry, maybe God will intervene and everything will be all right. On the school bus every morning I met the same people, played with them in the playground and for a while everything seemed normal. Then they found out about our situation and the slagging started: what is the best boy in the class going to do now? You'll have to leave this school, you can't stay in the area.

I found myself getting into more fights in the playground to defend my Dad's honour, until the situation became hopeless and I just trudged to and fro with some friends who were still willing to associate with me.

Again the call from upstairs.

"Where are my pills and bring me a cup of tea up."

As my mother disappeared up the stairs I surveyed the situation: the sitting room was empty, even the carpet was gone. There was plenty of floor space now for my train set. The wonderful train set I had got for Christmas and was made to put back in the box the next day because the engine came off the track and scratched one of our precious chairs. There were no chairs there now. I will put it down and play with it. I walked to the cupboard under the stairs where my toys were kept and opened the door, it was empty. At that moment my Mam arrived in the hallway.

"My train set Mammy, where is it?"

"I'm sorry, son. They've taken it." We both broke down and cried.

School Dinners
by Sandy Gee

The smell haunted the hall even when it was used for other things. And that smell had me sick each lunch time even in the queue before I got to the food itself. And the dinner ladies in their faintly frightening white aprons and hats – so remote and brusque – slapped it on the plate as you moved along. Then it was always grey-brown grainy meat with lumpy, half-round ice-cream scoop mash and more potatoes – blotchy brown roast ones – a splodge of pale, watery, long-lost-its-crunch cabbage and a thin sludge of gravy.

Was it always cold because I dawdled in my reluctance? The mashed potatoes were only a bland torture – find some not-so-lumpy bits to nibble. The roast potatoes nice-nasty – that rich brown oil-infused skin – but the oil was cheap, old and bitterly rancid. Cabbage that had so few intact cells it just dissolved into dishwater in the mouth.

I'd push it around and try and sit next to Mark Blakeborough who smelled but who ate others' leftovers.

Homesick
by Josie Darling

I felt homesick sometimes as a child, even when I was at home. It was a kind of stomach nausea when you miss people and a certain kind of warmth; it was a longing for everything to be all right, but you were not quite sure why they weren't. I still get the homesick feeling now I am grown up and I trust it to be completely real and can usually put it down to something, like not getting on with my partner for instance. However as a child I did not voice this feeling and felt I had to be polite and cheerful.

Around the age of eleven I was sent on a cycling holiday around the New Forest with a church group, who consisted of very well meaning but unfashionably dressed people. We had to stay in youth hostels and I hated it. I hated the scratchy blankets and the bunk beds with metal on and the forced jolliness of people cooking together in ugly saucepans. I hated the poring over maps of an evening and everyone wearing cagoules and Jesus sandals with socks. There were some other young people on the trip but I couldn't connect with them. I must have appeared an awkward and dreamy girl. My parents were splitting up at the time, but it was not talked about. and I think I felt like a squid or some other obscure underwater creature that no one quite knew what to do with.

What was I homesick for? Christmas trees and noisy siblings. Puddings like crème caramel or treacle tart. Mornings spent watching Harold Lloyd with a duvet over me. Rowing about in the river with a friend and pushing each other in. Pop music on the radio. The smell of cigarettes and beer. My mother reading to me. I don't know. Not being with these weirdos and having to enjoy myself, while my family were crumbling.

It was on one of the regular healthy trips out that I was cycling down a hill and I lost control. Of the bike I mean. Then I put the break on too hard and vaulted over the handlebars then went thump in the road. What a relief. I remember lying there and not being able to move. Thank God it's all over I thought. The nice Christians towered over me. Drivers slowed down to turn their heads and gaze at the bloodied child in the road. I've never had so much attention, I thought. I dimly heard an ambulance. I remember the reassuring voice of the men as they lifted me onto a stretcher and one said, "You've got nice eyebrows, love". I was elated by this remark.

I don't remember the hospital much, but later I was transferred to someone's house, a friend of my Mother's. She put me into her spare bedroom and it was impossibly neat. I lay in one of the twin beds and tried to behave like a pencil so I wouldn't make a messy lump and ruin the symmetry of the room. I drifted in and out of wonderful sleep. It was like the pleasure of when you can have a day off school for some minor cold, but amplified a hundred percent.

A few cuts and some concussion released me from the pain of trying to appear normal. I could give up.

My Introduction to the English
by Sanjay Kumar

I am the eldest son of first generation immigrants from the north-eastern state of West Bengal in the city of Calcutta in India. My father came to England in the early sixties to study, but my mother and I did not join him until much later and as a result my British education began relatively late in life.

When I entered Freda Gardham primary school in Rye I could only speak a few words of English. I found my classmates to be rather odd, was intrigued by wonderful things called shepherds pie and bangers and mash and was scandalised by the fact that the female teachers did not wear cotton saris and exposed their ankles when they walked. I was definitely a challenge for Mr Le Lacher and his wonderfully progressive team of educators at the school. Today I am a walking testament to their success in gently introducing me to Western culture and philosophy, the beauty and majesty of the language of Shakespeare and the awesome power of the written word. Above all they enabled me to harness the very best of my ancient Indian heritage with all that is great with modern European liberalism.

It was at primary school that I discovered my love of drama and theatrics which I developed further at university. My mother still has treasured photos of me in quite a few roles: as Chief Sitting Bull orchestrating the downfall of General Custer in the Battle of the Little Big Horn; as the evil King Herod in the Nativity play and as the bearded Captain Fido in the school play 'Robinson Curuso'. I remember that particular character very well because my moustache and beard blew off just as I was reaching the crescendo of my speech! It was only because I could see from the corner of my eye Ms Braeban and Ms Baldwin simultaneously mouthing the words 'Don't worry, it's alright – carry on. You're doing great!' that I continued, to the thunderous applause of the audience.

Even today when things go desperately wrong in daily life or I misjudge a situation with one of my work colleagues or I say or do something which hurts my partner or friends; I see, so clearly in my minds eye, the image those two exquisitely dressed, immaculately poised teachers mouth the words: 'Don't worry, it's alright – carry on. You're doing great!' One of the many things that Freda Gardham taught me was that a good teacher affects eternity; she can never tell where her influence stops.

My first day at the school is still very fresh in my mind. I was so nervous and busy clinging onto my mother's silk sari that I didn't realise that I was wearing my gym shoes instead of my normal black school shoes! It was also the day when I met a freckled boy of my age who would go on to become an excellent friend throughout my school years. His name was Craig Young and it was from him that I heard my first ever English ghost story - the story of the spirit of Old Freda haunting the school buildings. I have no doubt that this rites-of-passage tale is still being told and retold by pupils and former pupils today, wherever they may be.

Craig was also responsible for teaching me a game called football, which I never quite mastered, but I did successfully introduce him to chicken curry with roti bread.

When I look back to my time at Freda Gardham I always see the same image that comes from the deepest recesses of my mind: that of a small raven-haired, brown-skinned little boy looking at the world and God's universe with a sense of awe and wonder, and always, safely standing on the shoulders of giants. Giants that even today I am proud to call my first teachers.

There Was Snow Every Winter
by Richard Ince

When I was a child the snow was deep and you had to wear Wellington boots. Mine were always black. I liked wearing them. You could go into deep drifts and pretend you were an arctic explorer plodding along. You could slide on the ice and it didn't hurt your legs when you fell over. You had your long football socks and folded them over the top. That looked very stylish. It wasn't very nice though when we played snowball fights and one went inside your boot.

Wasn't it fun treading in thick mud, and the lovely rude squelching noises it made as you pulled your leg out?

Sometimes you borrowed your friend's boots, which were bigger than yours. They were loose. So you could kick out and the boot would go flying through the air and hit someone in the back

Last Communion
by Maggs Radcliffe

An enormous, lace-trimmed satin heart covered my little girl full-moon bum like a toaster cosy; devoid of taste, style and grace.

What was going through Mom's mind? Little girls aren't supposed to be decorated like wedding cakes in a cake-off competition. She had a sense of humour. I wanted simplicity, perfection and a hint of discretion regarding my first communion dress and accessories. Today was my lifetime commitment to the Grand Master. Only perfection would do as the ceremony commenced.

Sadly, nervousness consumed me like a child cycling for the first time without training wheels. Beautifully done up in satin, lace gloves blanketed my little hands. The dress was lovely, simple enough, as were all the external ornaments.

But. Butt - yes - what about that?

What if I tripped, stumbled? Fell down with dress flying high, unveiling a most bizarre nether region. What would the congregation think? A fetish fashionista? Or would they explode with delight, laughter and curiosity, hilariously concluding 'not everyone wears their heart on their sleeve...'

Best Friends
by Laila Raphael

My best friend Fiona thought she was a camel. So I said I would be a carrot.

Well, I know it's mad to say you are a carrot, but she really did seem to think, or at least make me believe, she was convinced she was a camel; and I always had to go one better. We were 11.

I suppose I was pretty desperate. We sat next to each other. Did I like her, or was I just in need of any company? She sat in the desk next to me, had long sandy coloured hair, a wiry body, angular jaw and the

teeth you get when you are seven and they have not arranged them-
selves properly yet.

I had recently returned from Israel, after being away for three years,
to a massive comprehensive in Essex. Making, having, losing friends,
discovering Jackie magazine, makeup, shoplifting from Woolworth's,
and my Gran's medical book which described the sexual act, yuck;
wanting to be Olivia Newton John, no chance.

Families also don't help sometimes; having a Dad on the front page
of the newspaper for drunk driving is a hard one to deny. It had to be
snotty Wendy Bowser with the perfect house who pointed it out to me
on the bus on the way to school, as if I did not know already. She seemed
to get some perverse pleasure out of being close to me and hating me at
the same time.

The girl I really liked and really got on with was Anne Grey who lived
in a council flat and liked Dave Edmunds and Peter Gabriel, and had
long feathered hair. But she sat next to J.C., the big mouthed, influen-
tial, popular bitch of the class, who did not like me. My friendship with
Fiona, who insisted on being called camel, only lasted as long as our
desks were stuck together. She headed for the desert and me to the hills
of Devon, our whole family, to try and escape our lives, our reputation.

I became friends with Julie Walsh, who wanted to be a funeral
director, Heather Mills who loved the band AC/DC and Angela Duncan
who was erring on the side of normal. Well, that's something.

Starting at St. Joseph's
by A.K. Andrew

I'd really been looking forward to starting school. Mum and I had
come up at the end of a school day and we had met Sister Finbar in the
playground as all the children were happily running out of the building.
What an enjoyable day it must have been for them I thought. The nun
who was to be my first teacher smiled kindly down at me, as I calmly
stood there holding Mum's hand.

"If she's half as good as her brother and sister she'll do very well at
St. Joseph's."

This was the first time I'd actually met a nun I think. Naturally I
had met priests who were always so nice to children and so close to
God. While I knew that nuns couldn't be as important as priests as they
were women, I thought they must be sort of angels-in training on earth. I
couldn't quite understand how they could all be married to Jesus. To my

five-year-old logic the angels–in training-scenario seemed pretty likely.

The Order at this school was Sisters of Mercy (or Sisters of No Mercy I later discovered). Sister Finbar had on the outfit still popular in the late 50's: black long sleeved ankle length robes, falling in pleats from the waist, with a belt and giant rosary tied around the middle.The large crucifix hanging from the end of the rosary was really impressive I have to say. Then there was the classic head attire: a black veil-like affair draping over the head and shoulders, stiffened at the front to keep its shape. Below that was a white head and neck guard, the purpose of which, I assume, was to render the head, forehead, ears, rear of the cheeks and entire neck invisible, thereby protecting the nuns from other people's unclean thoughts. To top off the ensemble was a giant white semi-circular bib that came half way down the chest. The real purpose of this bib was unclear to me, and while I knew it was not because they were really messy eaters, it has never been explained to me what it was for.

As well as looking forward to seeing these happy children and this kind angel-in-training again, going to school was probably my first milestone to be proud of, especially as I hadn't gone to kindergarten. It meant I was grown up – ok, not exactly, but at least it meant I was no longer a baby. Mum had told me how much I would enjoy it: playing with new friends, learning to read properly and do sums and everything. I already really enjoyed books, so I was anxious to start learning properly.

On that first day, I was starting to feel a bit twitchy as we approached the school gate. The word Girls was an integral part of the ironwork. Above it, carved in an arch of sandstone, were the words 'Saint Joseph's RC School'. There was suddenly a crush of too many children, none of whom I knew, and when Mum let go of my hand that was it. I could feel the panic rising.

"Bye-bye" she said, "Have a good first day and I'll see you at four o'clock."

As she bent to kiss me, I pulled back.

"Aren't you coming in with me? You promised you'd come to school with me, you promised," I whined.

"I know I did, but only to the school gates. You didn't think I'd be coming into the classroom with you did you?"

By now I could see that all the other Mums were saying their goodbyes at the gate, not even coming into the playground. I knew I was defeated, but didn't want to give up.

"Please Mum," I pleaded, "don't leave me alone." The children behind were pushing me. At this my lip started trembling. "I don't want to go in, I want to go home."

Her tone quickly changed. "Look here young lady, stop being such a baby. I'm going now."

The bell was ringing. She almost pushed me forward as she said goodbye. I slowly walked away from her, following the path of the other children. I turned to look back at her and she waved with a weak smile on her face. How could she be so mean?

As I entered the school building, jostled and fearful of the other children around me, there was not a friendly face in sight. Far from being the nice place with the lovely friends Mum had promised, this was a hideously grubby building that smelled of unwashed children, sawdust covered vomit and smelly plimsolls. This will be the last time I ever trust Mum again I thought sulkily.

Finally when I saw Sister Finbar my hopes were raised, but the face with the kindly smile was now graced with a dour look. She walked briskly through the classroom gruffly telling us to sit at one of the desks. These were double wooden desks, with flip up lids, inkwells and cast iron legs. She stood at the front of the class, holding a cane in her hand and said sternly "There will be no talking in my class. Those who do will be sorry. You can speak only when spoken to." I looked at the tiny window that was high above the blackboard wall at the front of the class and knew at that moment that the life of any child in her class was going to be a life filled with fear. I was not wrong.

Thirty years later I went for a trip down memory lane and took my lesbian partner past the school. (The nuns would have loved that.) It was in the process of being converted to a Muslim centre. There had been blue-bricks in the shape of a cross set into the high walls of the Catholic school building. Ordinary coloured brick was replacing these to render them invisible. At the Girls gate the arch sandstone that had said "Saint Joseph's RC School" was lying in broken pieces on the ground. Some of the letters were still intact. My partner climbed over the Girls gate and picked up the letter "A" for me.

Like my memory it's a bit crumbly, but I still have it.

boys in amber
by Anthony Spiers

we'll dwindle to rusty freckles
on a robin's egg
wear coats of warts and spectacles
made from the gold foil eyes of toads

when they call our names
we'll have fake names
troglodytes spirogyra
volvox

we won't smell of boys
but the rot of hawthorn blossom
our skin knurly
as oak bark

if they listen for us
we'll be mum as earthworms
or yaffle like woodpeckers
we'll crouch in the horse chestnut's toffee buds

we'll blush with chlorophyll
in nettlebeds
when they come for us
to make us into men

we'll be tangerine blots
on the bellies of newts
we'll hide under our own finger nails
they'll never find us

We Are Family

Finding the Strength
by Allison Clare

As I explore some of the people and places of my past and present, I am skirting round the real reason for my journey. In slowly unravelling the past, it is helping me to face a tragedy.

I moved away from Brighton for career reasons in the mid-nineties – I moved back at the beginning of 2006, trying to make a new start. However, suddenly my home town had become a city and my mother had been murdered in May 2002.

There is no escaping the fact that this has had a profound effect on me. Her second husband is serving a sentence for manslaughter, on the grounds of diminished responsibility. He was described as a 'wolf in sheep's clothing'. He stabbed Mum to death at 6am, but failed to call an ambulance until twelve midnight. During the eighteen hours that followed the stabbing, he moved her body, tried to stitch up the wound himself and attempted to resuscitate her with homemade shock pads.

With my aunt, her only sister, I sat through a three week trial at Lewes Crown Court, listening to excuse after excuse why this man had been slipping through the legal and medical net for years. His personality disorder, apparently untreatable, meant he was not able to be detained under the Mental Health Act. This man had been detained a month before the murder after stabbing Mum through the arm – she withdrew the charges. Nowadays the Crown Prosecution Service would have pushed ahead with a prosecution.

Following this you would have thought I would avoid abusive relationships. However, I fell into a similar trap, this time involving emotional and financial abuse. This resulted in me losing my home and having to move back to Brighton. As this situation is finally being resolved, I feel I have the strength to face the demons that led to the situation.

Pasta Days
by Valérie de Schaller

Mum always used to cook pasta on a Monday evening. This family tradition started because Monday was her assigned day to use the washing machine in the block of flats where we used to live in Switzerland.

Mum would also do all the housework on a Monday. She figured that by the time she'd washed all our clothes, dried and ironed them, and cleaned the flat from top to bottom, she deserved to cook only a simple meal. When I was old enough, she let me help her by ironing the easy stuff like tea-towels and Dad's hankies, checking on me while she cooked dinner and keeping an eye on my sister Stephanie.

The pasta, which alternated between spaghetti and "cornettes" – Swiss pasta in the shape of little horns – didn't take long, but the delicious tomato sauce she produced as an accompaniment was an art in itself.

I used to love seeing the huge heap of steaming pasta on the dinner table, with a large piece of butter melting on top. Unfortunately, the pasta was always followed by the daily salad – Mum's insistence that it was full of vitamins and must not be missed.

When we moved to England in 1981 and she owned a washing machine all to herself, Mum continued to do the housework on a Monday. So Monday was still pasta night.

These days I don't often cook pasta, maybe because eating it on my own isn't the same, but I do have salad every day.

Birthday Cake
by Margaret

I had a birthday cake. I was 12 or 14 — I think my mother sent it – it must have been after that time she came to see us. The time when I turned away from her with hate, saying 'Don't touch me'.

She said 'dahling' with that Irish brogue accent that I can't describe the sound of, I didn't want to go near her. It was 10 years after all since I had seen her.

I used to daydream and fantasise about it: Oh, when I see my mother I'll run up to her. I visualised an Our Lady figure or a beautiful lady silhouetted like on a cameo brooch, but I had waited too long and when she came I turned away. It was too late. Although perhaps not, because I have never forgotten she said I had piano fingers and I later tried to learn the piano.

Anyway I got this cake, the first cake I had ever had, and I secreted it away. I left it in the dormitory in its box under my bed. When I went back to it (probably days later), it had been eaten by mice and had to be thrown away.

Perhaps by not eating the cake and secreting it away I was refusing love. I think I still turn away and don't trust in others.

Let the Dust Settle
by Josephine

I never really appreciated just how much my Mum has given us until I had children of my own. Having children has been the best thing I have ever done and with it I acquired a desire to make sense of my own chaotic '70s childhood. This is my story, my version of events, but it also involves other people, which is why I have changed names until they are ready to share their stories.

Madness entered my childhood home through the back door and never really left. It accumulated like dust in the dark corners of the house; there if you looked closely, but largely ignored. But periodically the atmosphere would change. The air became charged with a crazed energy as my mother paced from room to room in her manic mission of the moment. Nights became days; anger turned to laughter; coffee a substitute for food.

As a teenager I would try to ignore her night prowling. I would curl up in bed with my arm hiding my face and pretend I was fast asleep. Sometimes it worked, other times I was forced to respond as I couldn't bear the silent tears at the end of my bed. Occasionally I would wake to the smell of a hospital ward: my mother had spent the dark hours bleaching the house of germs. If she'd had a particularly active night I would discover that half my clothes had disappeared.

"Mum, what have you done with my clothes? I'm late for school."

"It doesn't matter dear - you don't need them."

"What are you talking about Deborah?"

Somehow I thought that by using her first name I could take control of the situation – get her to behave.

"It's alright, darling. I've been creating my funeral pyre – widow's black. I am a volunteer – you know I won't take any money."

My brother Sam and I would search the house and discover in Deborah's bedroom a pile of black clothes neatly folded in the middle of the room.

"Deborah why are you doing this? I can't stand it. What's wrong with you?" I spotted my school skirt and pulled it from the bottom, causing the pyramid to tumble - my Mum looked visibly distressed. Her night's work undone.

"It's ok Jo, just leave it all to me. I'll sort this all out. It won't be long now. I need to finish the pyre. Don't worry, I'll make sure everything is all ok for you both."

I turn away from her in despair but just as quickly as she slipped into madness she comes full circle to play the dutiful mother.

"Have you completed your maths homework?"

"Yes."

"Well show it to me."

"Why are you suddenly so interested in what I'm up to?"

"Because education is the most valuable treasure you will ever have."

"I'm late for school."

"Josephine, I would like to see your maths homework before you go." On my way out I showed her my half finished algebra. But although it was only minutes since we had last spoken – she had slipped away again. "Next door have stolen part of the house."

"Mum, what are you talking about?"

"Listen, you can hear the banging now."

"So what?"

"I can see through the window that they've put in an extra room. How do you think they've done that – they've stolen it from us."

"Mum, don't be ridiculous."

"Our house has got smaller."

"Just stop this. They must have knocked down a couple of walls in their own house to create more space. "

"Shush. Don't shout. Keep your voice down, they can hear you, Josephine."

"I'm not SHOUTING. Of course they can't hear us."

"Listen. They're at it again."

And the conversation would fast deteriorate as my mother descended further into the treadmill of her paranoia. But on my way out of the house I couldn't resist looking at the wallpaper for signs of disturbance. Could you catch madness?

Of course, her craziness was always better than her silence. Sometimes there would be hours when she said next to nothing.

"Mum – would you like something to eat?

"You must be really hungry, what about some toast or a banana? Mum did you hear me? How about a cup of tea?

"Mum, please just say something. I'm getting really fed up with this. You're frightening Sam."

Deborah continued to fiddle with the gold band she still wore on her left hand. She had barely eaten for weeks and the ring almost slipped off her finger. She eventually looked up at me, willing herself to speak.

"It's alright, darling. Let me get you some food. I wonder what I've got," her voice trailed off.

When we were younger, my grandparents would immediately step in and look after us at the first signs of erratic behaviour. The doctors would pack Deborah off for a couple of months to the nearby psychiatric hospital, a large, rambling Victorian institution. While we hated her going there, it generally had a calm and caring atmosphere. In many ways it was a true asylum where she could paint, walk in the gardens, and have time and help to restore her energies and mental equilibrium before returning home. Years later they pulled it down and built a chocolate box housing estate, leaving only an overstretched hospital ward to cater for those who really could no longer cope with their lives. There were no extensive gardens or flower arranging, just heavy doses of drugs, locked doors and the occasional electric shock treatment.

As we grew older, Sam and I thought we could make her better. We would cover for her as long as possible; make up excuses to our grandparents, family friends and well meaning but ineffectual social workers. Of course we were as deluded as her. Once the mania had set in, it was impossible to stop – she was on a mission and we were mere bystanders.

Yet even in the depths of these mad bad days, we sometimes felt we had stepped into a black comedy where we had no choice but to laugh. My mother could have a wicked sense of humour and in her colourful, outlandish outfits she knew how to work the crowds. We, her sensible children, became minor characters in her plot.

"Jo, I've decided to sell this house and get a much bigger one."

"Why do you want to do that? Anyway we can't afford it."

Although only 14 years old, I was very aware of money and the lack of it in our household - particularly when my mother went on manic spending sprees. She filled the house with great bargains – four pairs of blue flip flops size 3 that fitted none of us; typewriters that no longer worked; a job lot of second hand Levi jeans (which Sam and I fought over).

"We could move Nanny and Granddad, Aunty Rose and Uncle Terry down here and start a family theatre."

"What are you talking about? I'm not even going to discuss this with you."

"I would be the director and the main lead. You and Sam can act in it after you get back from school - it'll be good for your education. Nanny and Granddad could run front of house, and Aunty Rose and Uncle Terry – well they can sell ice creams. Those Cornettos – nothing common. Of course, we would need to employ the odd professional actor – but they would love it down here – next to the sea."

And then Deborah flounced off and came back dressed in a deep bottle green velvet evening dress with lace sleeves, a wide brimmed blue hat with a peacock feather and holding a small red and white flag that should have been sitting on top of a sandcastle. She took a deep bow and started to sing.

"Oh, I do like to be beside the seaside. Oh, I do like to be beside the sea... Come on Jo, join in. Here, wave the flag."

"No thanks."

"Where the brass bands play – tiddly om pom pom."

Despite my annoyance, I started to giggle. It was all so awful but at the same time you couldn't help but laugh. Deborah gave me that look which said she knew exactly what was going on and started to laugh with me.

"You are funny, Mum."

"Oh yes, I know. Hi-lar-i-ous. Lah di dah dah dah. Pom di pom, pom, pom. I can't remember any more can you?"

"No – sorry."

"Jo, you know I didn't really mean it."

"What's that?"

"The theatre idea."

"I know you didn't - but it made me laugh at least."

"Thanks for listening."

"It's all right, Mum."

"You aren't worried about me are you?"

"Of course I'm not." I looked away from her.

But in the end her frenzy of ideas and exploits exhausted us. Sam and I couldn't keep up with her and we retreated to the sidelines. Inevitably we – her family – became her betrayers. I, as the oldest, was Judas.

"Jo, who's that knocking at the door?"

"I think it's Dr Gordon. We called him."

Deborah was absolutely furious with us. "I told you we don't need him – there is nothing wrong with me. Just ignore him. Don't you dare answer the door."

"But we do need him Mum – you know you're not feeling well. And we're so tired 'cos you keep waking us up in the night."

"Please Jo, don't let him in. I don't want to leave you both."

As I opened the door to the doctor I could hardly speak to him. My throat felt so tight it hurt as I tried to hold back the tears. As doctors go he was pretty kind and understanding, although at that moment he felt like the enemy.

"Don't worry. You've done the right thing."

I led him slowly into the front room filled with the manic debris of the previous few weeks. Deborah now sat quietly on our red put-u-up sofa. On her lap sat a small plastic bag barely filled with her basic needs – a toothbrush, bar of soap and nightie. She knew the game was up.

"Hello Deborah, I hear you're not very well. Would you like me to find out if there are any beds available at the hospital?"

"Please doctor."

"I think it's for the best."

"Of course. I'm very tired Doctor, but I'm really worried about Josephine and Samuel. They are such good children." Deborah's voice was barely a whisper, she was disappearing before us.

"Don't worry, your mother will be here soon and she's going to look after them for a couple of weeks while you have a rest."

We sat quietly for the next hour, too exhausted to even pretend to make polite conversation. Then the atmosphere changed as my Grandmother arrived, all bustle and good intentions. She hid her grief behind a big smile and cups of sweet tea and ham sandwiches that lay untouched on the square oak table in the corner of the room. My solid, silent Grandfather reassured us with hugs and Fox's Glacier Mints from his deep pockets.

We heard the ambulance pull up outside and Deborah got up stiffly. She held Sam and I really tightly in her arms with her eyes screwed shut. Then she rushed outside and got straight into the vehicle, holding nothing but the plastic bag. She never looked back to see the falling tears and the dust begin to settle.

Aunt Edith
by Josie Darling

I am seven and a half. My name is Josie but people call me JoJo or Josephina Semolina Pudding. Today we are going to visit Auntie Edith. She is really my great aunt and she's a bit scary but I really like her.

I would even quite like to live with her, as she would never notice what you did, but her house is so dirty and messy. She smells funny; she smokes these cigarettes called Weights, and she smells of spicy knickers and delicious cigarettes. She has ginormous bosoms, like long floppy ears, they hang down to her knees nearly. Some people call them boobs or knockers or bust. She wears sort of silky patterned dresses which stop by her knees and she always has lace up shoes and her feet are a funny shape like knobbly rocks. Sometimes she spits when she talks and she has some grey porridgy stuff in the corner of her mouth which never goes away. I like her though because she likes me.

When she stays at our house I get into her double bed with her in the morning and play cards and my Mum brings her breakfast in bed, and I like her funny smell. She has such a loud voice and it's ever so posh. When she comes to visit us she shouts at the harbour master, "IAN," and he calls back, "Coming Ede".

She makes me laugh 'cos she doesn't care what people think of her. Everybody likes my Auntie Edith. My Mum says she is a character. I don't know what this means. Auntie Edith lives in Stepney and helps poor people. Once she brought ten girls to stay with us for a week with a strange man called Oscar Tapper. He was a bit like Willy Wonker with black clothes and pointy shoes. These girls were from the East End and they said "bu h er" instead of butter so I tried to copy them and they taught me lovely songs.

Anyway, today we are going to London so we go on the train then the bus. The bus is red and dangerous 'cos you can step on or off when it's moving and it's so big and there are lots of black people and Indian people and I'm not used to seeing them so I stare at them. When we get to Auntie Edith's flat it's all dark and she makes me a cup of tea and one for my Mum too. I can't drink mine 'cos I know the cup is dirty and it makes me feel sick just looking at it.

Mrs Gutteridge's Nuts
by Rob Stride

Mrs Gutteridge was my friend's Nan and she lived in a flat at the top of Coronation Fields. She was funny and kind, but as mad as a box of frogs.

One day I was at my friend's house, 96 Great Elm Road, (I lived and was born at 92, so this was a handy friendship, we didn't like each other that much, but our parents got on so we made an effort). The cheap doorbell rang and Nanny Gutteridge appeared with smiling face, old hands and a walking stick.

She was made comfortable and my friend's Dad put James Last on the Boots stereo. He had lots of James Last's records, box sets, *Readers' Digest* editions, and he was always playing them on his poxy *Boots* stereo.

"Did you like those brazils?" shouted Nan Gutteridge. "Did you like those brazil nuts? Did you eat them?"

"Yes," said the whole family.

"Yeah, they were lovely Mum," said young Mrs Gutteridge. "We ate them watching Dragnet last night."

"Only like the chocolate," said Nan.

"What?" said young Mrs Gutteridge

"Only like the chocolate, shame to waste the nuts. Glad you liked them."

In Praise of Grandmothers
by Allison Clare

I want to write about two amazing guiding lights in my life. Nana Win was so houseproud that relatives used to call her council flat 'the palace'; whereas Grandma Florence's maisonette in north London was always chaotic, full of books, magazines and projects on the go.

These two very different women were my strongest female role-models as a child due to my difficult relationship with my parents. Nana Win had an amazing way with people and would send you 'ooffle dust', like fairy magic, to help things succeed or get better if you were ill. Whereas Grandma Florence's strength of character was formidable. These two very different women have certainly been here for me, even after their deaths, throughout my life.

As a child, I spent as much time away from my parental home as I could. One of my bolt-holes was the north London home of my feisty Grandma Florence Gertrude.

Originally from Bodmin in Cornwall, she moved to London at a young age to go into service. Then she moved on to work for the *Co-Op*, where she didn't look back. Florence eventually became manageress for the cosmetics department in the Camden Town branch. After she had two daughters she continually improved her education and attended the Robert Owen College founded by the *Co-Op*.

Both my parents had literacy difficulties and there were no books around at home. The only real 'culture' in our house was in the bottom of the fridge! I was so fortunate that Grandma kept me supplied with books at her house. One of my earliest memories is her letting me sit up to read The Hobbit. In later years she made sure I read 1984 and Brave New World. She also introduced me to classical music like the Planets Suite by Holst.

Although Grandma was keen for me to advance my reading skills, when it came to some novels, she would censor them. For example, she tore out pages from some D.H. Lawrence novels that involved sex. It recently dawned on me that she must have read them herself to do this! Although she came across as a very strong feminist, she wasn't without her warmth. My poor Grandad had long since been banished to another bedroom, and much to his disgust Grandma would frequently have her 'foreign' neighbours around the house. She often seemed more at home in the Asian community.

Florence was a true socialist, never believed in property ownership and strongly advocated for access to education, particularly for women. She put away a pound a month for both myself and my female cousin to help us go to college. Through her connections with the education committee of the *Co-Op*, we travelled together to East Germany and Czechoslovakia in 1979. It was a tour to celebrate the 30th anniversary of the German Democratic Republic – a unique experience for a twelve year old girl from Whitehawk.

My beautiful Nana, Winifred May, lived in Essex Place, a high rise block in Kemp Town. I often spent time at her eighth floor flat and watched the Marina being built from there. We would walk down to the seafront, along to the original Peter Pan playground. You could take turns on a makeshift stage in talent competitions. I remember singing 'In Dublin's Fair City – alive, alive O.' (It was the original forerunner to the X-factor!).

Our route down to the playground was often via Duke's Mound, a series of pathways, mostly under trees, leading down from the top main road to the beach. Nana would say, "Make sure you take big steps down the path because you don't want to tread on the fairies."

Looking back, I am now certain my Nana had picked up on the fact that even in those days this was a popular place for gay men to meet. As I later discovered my Nan was very non-judgemental about diverse lifestyles and her fairy stories now bring back happy memories.

my father's pin-up girl
by Anthony Spiers

in the barber garden I'm trussed
in an old bedsheet as my father mows
the small brown lawn of my head

his open-air salon
has no queues no mirrors
no candy-striped red and white pole

though there are scarlet flowers
on his runner beans to watch and white tails
of bumble bees rummaging in the pollen

now hungry clippers nibble round my ears
and as he rakes the cuttings with his comb
I'm not peeping into the future

where other boys wear fantastic haircuts
light years away from this
my prickly short-back-and-sides

for I'm having a good look
at the pencil box where my father stashes
his barber tools

which sports a photo of the Venus de Milo
goddess of the things
he and I will never speak about

Teenage Kicks

Excess
by Julian Harvey

Backstage at the Marquee, Wardour Street, with the Bollock Bothers. A night of drinking and smoking. I walked up and down a road in Maida Vale, trying to remember where my brother's flat was.

First Kiss
by Sandy Gee

It was Anita's party. Her parents were out. We had lots of cider and lots of boys. But somehow, before I'd realised what was happening, we'd gone from games, to everyone paired up, snogging and groping each other on the chairs round the edge of the room in the semi-dark.

How could I be the only one left?

I was gutted and desperate. I had no idea what to do with myself so I kept going into the kitchen and filling my glass again – every 60 seconds. It went on forever. Until…

I was coming out of the kitchen yet again and a boy, temporarily separated from his snogging partner (who happened to be my best friend Sharon), was coming in. We literally bumped into each other and – did I really? I think I was desperate enough – but did I grab and lunge at him?

In any case we were soon with the other couples on chairs at the side of the room. I was hungrily grabbing this experience for all it was worth. I was going to come out of this an experienced kisser. Wet tongue. Virtually chewing my lips off, sucking my whole lips and tongue into his mouth – this boy was experimenting too.

And in my avid eagerness to no longer be a kissing virgin I was indiscriminate – I seized it all.

Gnostic Sandwiches
by Ged Duncan

When I was fifteen I only had one pair of jeans and they had gone through the seat and the knees – about ten years before it was fashionable. My own fashion statement was elastoplast. I had fetching nude brown plasters stuck over the holes.

There were two problems with this method of repair. After a period of sitting it was common to find the jeans stuck to my bottom and their subsequent removal excruciating. And the patches curled up at the edges quickly becoming dirty and skanky, but somehow retaining potent adhesive properties.

Kevin's Mum was not pleased one day when I rose to find several tassels from her new settee stuck to my rear.

But don't misunderstand me. We were not poor. In fact things were going quite well for my Dad at work. Guess a teenager has to find some way to rebel, and this was mine. Mum died a thousand deaths every time I went out in those jeans.

As a teenager, of course, I knew it all. My particular brand of precocious wisdom was homespun syncretism which might be called 'gnostic anarchism'. What's that, you ask? I didn't believe in property, I gave my money to anyone I felt needed it…and I knew that ice creams and toast racks were icons of middle-class decadence. God told me so.

So I went to Kevin and said. 'We need to feed the hungry. Let's go to Brighton beach and give sandwiches to the homeless.'

Kevin was clever and liked the logistical challenges presented by this proposal. We had little money and the scheme was unlikely to meet with parental approval. In his family caravan he found a jar of jam, which he brought round to my house with as much sliced white bread as he could liberate from home without detection.

The jam was covered by a thick layer of mould which we scraped off and put in the garden under the lupins. We thought the removal of butter would be noticed, so we spread the jam on the bread without it. It made a couple of rounds. Not enough to end poverty and hunger in Brighton and Hove.

So we pooled our financial resources, visited the grocers round the corner and bought six slices of reconstituted ham. We spread it thinly on more bread, taken this time from my family's breadbin, and laid the sandwiches in an empty Christmas Assortment tin. That's better. That may even feed five thousand.

We didn't need bike locks because we had guardian angels. Though we did help them a bit by hiding our cycles behind the beach huts near Hove Lagoon. I had cycled with the Christmas Assortment tin under my arm, which meant that the loose sandwiches had rearranged themselves, subtly remixing processed ham, mouldy jam and bits of bread, now soggy and disintegrating. But we reassembled them artfully and we were sure that the homeless would still be grateful.

Neither of us wanted to admit how nervous we were now we had arrived. An orderly queue of needy, grateful people had not appeared despite both the epicurean aroma emanating from our tin and the compassionate half-smiles on our faces. The setting sun threw long shadows from the iron railings edging the beach and dog walkers and joggers passed on the promenade. We may have been a bit early for homeless bedtime.

We decided we would walk towards the West Pier, underneath which, we had been told, a passable night could be spent by those without a home. As we walked we eyed anyone who was neither jogging nor clutching a dog-leash.

'What about him?' I hissed. As we passed a middle-aged man wearing a dirty raincoat. We circled round, pretending to watch the herring gulls flying out to sea after a days scavenging.

'He's got a pink paper under his arm,' said Kevin.

'So?'

'*Financial Times.*'

Kevin was doing an Economics 'O' Level and I deferred to the fact that he had obviously been trained to identify businessmen and investors.

These assessments continued as we strolled towards the Pier with our biscuit tin. We tried to be inconspicuous but received several glares, one Wot you lookin at? and an enticing smile from a girl about our age.

When we took the path under the West Pier we found only one person – a bored looking policeman.

'Alright lads?' he said, as he saw us loitering.

We suddenly felt guilty. With our hidden sandwiches suspiciously oozing jam and criminality.

'Wouldn't hang around here. Been told to keep the place clear. 'Keep the hobos away,' they said, though God knows where else they've got to go.'

There was no alternative but to continue purposefully and innocently along the lower promenade towards the Palace Pier. It was now nearly dark and a cold breeze was blowing from the sea, misting our skin and our clothes with salty moisture. I was getting hungry and wishing I had worn a coat.

'Fancy a sandwich?' I asked Kevin.

We agreed to eat the jam ones as they were the most manky and sat on a bench chewing without relish. We nobly saved the quality processed ham ones for the homeless, though the bread had gone pink due to jam seepage.

'Look,' said Kevin suddenly, pointing to a man in his twenties who had a blanket wrapped round his shoulders and two carrier bags at his feet. More tellingly, he was eating cold chips directly from a waste bin.

We looked at each other and without speaking stood together and marched towards him with the Christmas Assortment tin carried in front of us like a sacrament.

'Would you like a sandwich mate?'

'Fuck off.'

'We just made them...er, they're nice,' I said, without conviction.

The man looked in our tin, then tentatively lifted the edge of one of the sandwiches. But suddenly he flinched, jumped backwards and crashed into the bin, which fell over, spilling rubbish onto the ground.

'Fuck off, you bastards!'

'What's wrong?' We were aware that our cuisine was lacking in certain respects, but his reaction seemed a bit extreme.

'Meat is Murder!' he shouted.

We stood, speechless. Kevin looked at the ground. I wiped some jam from my chin with my sleeve.

'Piss off, murderers,' said the man. He turned his back to us, squatted down amongst the fallen rubbish and resumed his meal.

It was hard not to feel disheartened. We crunched down across the beach and sat on a bank of shingle facing the sea. It was a clear night and a quarter moon was rising over the water. The salty wind stung our faces. We huddled together for warmth and began to tell each other jokes to cheer ourselves up.

As I was laughing heartily about the one with the nun in the bath, a dark pile of shingle a little way down the beach grunted, and then morphed into a huge figure. Someone had been asleep on the beach and we had woken him up.

The figure pounded through the pebbles towards us. Already we could see he was huge, the moonlight catching the tangled hairs of a magnificent, greying beard that reached his chest, his long, damp hair swinging as he strode. We could only wait - there was no time to run.

When he stood between us and the sea all we could see was the darkness of his bulk.

'Excuse me,' he said in a cut-glass public school voice. 'Could you lend me ten pee?'

Christopher silently ate all our sandwiches without complaint and it was us who felt grateful.

'Where do you sleep?' he asked me when he had finished, eyeing the elastoplast on my jeans and the jam stains on our jumpers.

'Oh, we...we're not...I mean..'

'At home. In bed,' said Kevin, rescuing me.

'Nice. This is my bed,' he said pointedly, patting the shingle.

He looked straight at me and it was disconcerting to notice that I could see white all around his irises. In the moonlight pale crumbs from our sandwiches twinkled in his beard.

'Do you live in a big house?' he asked, still staring straight at me.

I could see where this was going, and so could Kevin. We had a wordless conversation involving parents, wide-eyed vagrants, doorstep arguments and being grounded for a very long time. At the end of this silent exchange we looked at each other and said just one word.

'Benny.'

Benny was part of our radical gang, but he was twenty three. Although it was treacherous from an ideological perspective we were glad, at that moment, that he had just bought a house. We were even ready to forgive his other bourgeois act – he and Jane had just got married.

It was a long walk to Poet's Corner from near the Palace Pier, especially as we collected our bikes on the way. But Christopher tagged along quite happily, stopping frequently to ask people to lend him ten pee.

It was ten o'clock when we reached Benny's house and the only light on was in the bedroom. A long time passed before he came to the door with a frown and a subsiding bulge in his underpants.

'Who is it?' Jane called from upstairs.

When Benny told her the bedroom door slammed.

I had not got on well with Jane since their wedding the month before when I had given them a humorous 'In Deepest Sympathy' card and a plastic sieve from *Woolworths*.

Benny quietly ushered the three of us into the living room and we sat down on the available boxes and cushions. He and Jane had just managed to buy the run-down house, but didn't yet have the means for furnishing or decoration.

'What the hell do you want?'

We introduced him to Christopher and told him how we met. A faint dawning of comprehension appeared on Benny's face.

Christopher just stared at Benny. He had developed a strong twitch and was muttering quietly to himself.

Jane knocked fiercely on her floor, our ceiling.

There followed a long cryptic conversation. The gist of this was, 'If you think he is staying here tonight you are out of your minds. But how the fuck are we going to get him out of the house.'

Of course, being rather literal, Kevin and I were being slow on the uptake. Christopher, on the other hand, understood perfectly.

'Sometimes,' he said suddenly, interrupting our exchanges. 'Sometimes, when p..people really annoy me...I have to harm them.'

We became very quiet.

'You're really annoying me now!'

He began to mutter again, almost as if he was arguing with himself, and then stood up and advanced towards Benny with his arm raised and his hand open ready for a karate chop.

Then he collapsed on the floor and started to have a fit.

Christopher did get a bed for the night...in Brighton General Hospital. Benny eventually returned to his bed with Jane. And Kevin and I got back to our homes very late.

'I've been at Benny's,' I said by way of explanation, which was true. 'And we forgot the time because we were having a laugh,' which was not. It was more difficult to explain the sticky Christmas Assortment biscuit tin and the jam stains on my clothes.

But I escaped with a minor grounding. And the following week, when I got my pay packet from my Saturday job, I bought a new pair of jeans.

Journey
by Yvonne Luna

I remember the Paris-Geneva night train that had no couchettes. I was 19, or was it 20, heading back to my hotel management college in Lausanne, reputedly the best in the world: cost my Mother an arm and leg to get me there, up that ladder. And here was I, moving to switch off the light as the Asian family in our carriage seemed to be already asleep, and the young man opposite from me very far from asleep.

I don't remember a single word passing between us. I had no idea what his voice sounded like, what language he spoke, what country he was from.

I don't remember how I reacted after he climaxed, something which happened within seconds of us touching. A nervous cough made me question how asleep the Asians were. I don't remember how dark it was, nor whether there were any glimpses of light through which our silent mating could be watched.

I don't remember the expression on his face as he left the train at his destination ahead of mine, at which I alone broke the silence: "When will I see you again? When will…"

It's Off to Work We Go

First Job
byJudith Greenfield

The world of Forestal Land Timber and Railways was my introduction to full time working. I was one of the few from my college class who ventured further afield for employment. My 45 minute train journey to London started with a frantic bicycle ride across Ascot racecourse, down the stairs, through the tunnel that stretched out under the racetrack, up the stairs again, lugging the bike with me. Then I would freewheel down the hill to the station, throw the bike in the general direction of the bike shed and jump onto the train as it was leaving. A few weeks after I'd been there one of the spinster-like secretarial women types took me to one side and very politely gave me a short discourse on personal hygiene. I'm not surprised. I must have been very unfragrant after my sprint to work each morning.

The job was boring. My boss was boring. The company was a remnant of the old colonial days, so out of date. The timber and railways had gone and only the land was left. My boss hadn't had a secretary before and I hadn't been one yet so there I was sat in the corner of his vast stale smelling oak lined room, neither of us quite knowing what was expected of us. My desk contained the bare essentials and I recall spending hours typing the same thing out over and over again just to fill the time and look busy. I spent quite a lot of my days there in the postal room. There was a uniformed postal hierarchy and the Major took me under his wing and found bits and pieces for me to do, franking post and making parcels. Lunch time in Fleet Street was heaven after my stuffy mornings and the lemon cream cake at Lyons Corner House was a gastronomic joy I can still taste even after so many years.

I was totally horrified one day when my boss asked me to stay late to finish something which to him was very important. By 5.30 my tedium was so great that the thought of having to stay even later made me burst into tears in front of him. I didn't stay there much longer. It wasn't for me at all, my one venture into a proper full time office job.

Funnily enough, a few years later I was sent on a temping job to BOC at Hammersmith. Sitting waiting for my appointment who should appear across the foyer but that old boss from FLTR. I put the name and face together, 2 and 2 actually did make 4. As soon as he turned away from me I quietly stood up and made a quick exit from the building.

Best Job (1)
by Rob Stride

I ended up working with one of James Last's singers, Kay Garner. She had been one of Dusty's backing vocalists in the 60's – she had a hit with her lead vocals on *Cerrones – super nature*. Kay had backed almost every solo singer in Britain during the 60's and 70's and had dated a "Four Season".

Once she sang 'Cry Me a River' at the piano just for me while we were having a break from recording.

I wanted to kiss her feet.

I Don't Belong Here
by Maggs Radcliffe

Bloody fingers burning…dammit.

I was sick and tired of paper cuts from eight hours of filing. Never – I mean never – apply for work at a Collection Agency. You start at the bottom, literally, on your knees, arms overloaded with manila folders full of strangers' financial trials and tribulations.

Voices of the professional collectors (AKA legal criminals) lying day after day to retrieve pertinent info out of unsuspecting debtors in order to garnish their wages if, in fact, they were employed in the first place. Bragging about mastering the art of deception and who trapped the largest catch of the day. I go-phered their coffee as well when I wasn't nursing my fingers and wiping blood off the files.

"Want sugar with that?" I'd scream at the line lizards.

Let's see now, where did I put the rat poison

Best Job (2)
by Malcolm Williams

My first job was when I was still at school. I worked in Harvey's Brewery and they had to put me in the van or get a taxi to take me home.

Yes, you got it. I was drunk everyday. I cannot remember a lot about it. To my mates at school, it was the best job ever.

Interview at W H Smith
by Julian Harvey

It was like a scene from Trainspotting. I wolfed on about nothing in particular. They looked at me as if I had just stepped off a flying saucer.

The Jumper
by Ty Galvin

One of the things not well known about the Brighton Pier is the use made of it by people looking to end their lives. They were commonly referred to as "jumpers". As a result, usually two of the security staff were also qualified lifeguards. Extending nearly six hundred yards into the sea, the end of the Pier can be remote and foreboding in the early hours of the morning.

On a summer's morning during my time there as an electrician, I went in very early to do some emergency work before it opened for business. It was at the extreme end of the pier and I had the whole place to myself and the seagulls. That was until I looked up from the cable I was repairing to see a man in his thirties leaning over the railings and staring vacantly at the sea.

"Oh my God, it's a jumper."

My thoughts of ignoring him and getting on with my work quickly vanished. What could I do? I was all alone with no hope of help for some time. I had to engage him. I was not a good enough swimmer to go in after him if he went and I mentally noted that the nearest lifebuoy was some distance away.

That summer dolphins had been seen off the end of the Pier and I decided to use this as an introduction.

Quietly making my presence felt so as not to startle him, I said, "Come to see the dolphins have you?"

"Fuck off, I'll be with them in a minute," was the terse reply.

I carried on regardless. "Oh, I believe it's a pleasant experience swimming with dolphins".

"I can't swim," he snapped back at me, while throwing one leg over the railing. He was now precariously poised over the edge. Even if he changed his mind he would have to be helped back carefully.

"Why are you doing this?" I asked.

"I've lost everything, my business went bust and my wife left me". He babbled on, "I started from nothing and built it up and then the financial institutions lost all my money". It was a time of the stock market collapse.

I must keep talking to him, surely someone is due in now.

"You're a young man and you can do it all again, but not from forty feet under the sea", I said.

Just then I noticed two security men creeping up behind him and I kept his attention towards me with anything that came into my head so that they could grab him before he realized they were there. This they succeeded in doing and the last I saw of him was being led away, protesting vehemently.

I carried on with my work that day, thinking 'Did I do the right thing? What did he have in store, poor bastard?' Although other people praised my actions, I was reluctant to congratulate myself.

Some months later, I was working under the Pier when a colleague said I was required up top. I climbed up to see the "jumper" standing there, where I had encountered him that fateful morning.

He had a pleasant looking lady with him and he stuck out his hand to me. "This is my wife, she wanted to meet you".

She leaned forward and hugged me as she said in a low voice, "We have re-started our lives and we're on the up again".

He then handed me a parcel, saying "I'm in the leather trade and I have had this made for you. I knew your size. As a matter of fact I will never forget your size".

At my tea break I opened it – it was an exquisite hand made jacket. And yes, it fitted me perfectly.

The Apprentice
by David Boxall

Festooned like stars, the cobwebs hung.
The dark bare earth floor waited, cold.
My eyes, still dazzled by the sun,
Although a boy's, felt ages old.
The air was stale like last week's bread.
Smelt oak sawn, damp as a wet child.
White fleshless ribs, untreated dead,
Awaited elm planks from the wild.
Malleable smelly sap infused
Yet strong as every Sussex tree.
Only selected timber used.
I'd think "this boat's like part of me".
Then throw the great doors open wide
To let morning come tumbling in
The slipway lacking wind and tide
Muddier than a refuse bin
Smells like a pub at closing time
But...this was my old working place.
And I'm a worker, that's no crime.
To lay about is a disgrace.
And so I set to, copper nails
Roves and dolly at the ready.
Then in the governor slowly sails
Old as a tree, half as sturdy,
Patient. Honest. One of the few.
Sonny they called him, but not me.
He gladly taught me all he knew.
And now he's only history.
Home was a cycle ride away.
A cup of tea. A future dream.
A spring board to another day.
A blood soaked shirt without a seam.

Home Sweet Home

Shouting at Seagulls
by Allison Clare

During a particularly bleak time, my friend of thirty years said she would love me even if I was one of those women 'on the seafront shouting at seagulls'.

We are both Brighton girls and have often discussed writing about our experiences. *Salt & Vinegar* has given me the first opportunity to start on this journey. So time has come to dip my toes in the Banjo Groyne waters again. Brighton is more than a dirty postcard destination, it's home. Beneath the veneer there are some wonderful people and places: here are two.

Nora, one of the amazing, inspirational individuals in Brighton, has been mentioned briefly in The Cheeky Guide to Brighton. I was keen to meet Nora again, and a rainy Monday in July gave me such an opportunity. Charging up St James Street with her trolley recently emptied, her lipstick was, as ever, immaculate. As we bump into each other she remembers our last chat almost a year ago, even down to my star sign.

This woman is worth more than a brief mention in a tourist guide. Her mission is to feed the birds of the city. Nora's assertion is that man is over-fishing the sea so the gulls are coming further inland to feed. Nora obtains the food from skips behind supermarkets, not only bread, but also soup and butter, anything basically to feed her friends. Although her efforts are not always appreciated by the authorities, she continues undeterred. With her beautiful spirit of determination, for me she is a strong symbol of Brighton, where individuality is still just tolerated. As we are chatting, both getting drenched, I offered her a cuppa. She said she was busy but left with the comment, "At least, I won't have to wash my jacket today."

At almost 81 years old, I hope Nora long continues to shout at seagulls and continues her one-woman campaign against environment damage by man. Next time we shout at seagulls raiding our bins, we should consider the reasons.

Now I want to take you to the home of the Gutbuster. Having unconventional sleep patterns need not be a problem in Brighton. One of my favourite places over the years is the all night café on Circus Street. Earlier in the night, you encounter the wonderful post-club philosophers, mainly students, with other 'unconventional' nocturnals thrown in. Towards dawn, taxi drivers and lorry drivers drift in. Occasionally you can spy other nocturnal walkers with their minders or drivers.

Later people obviously living out of bags stumble in. Everyone's equal in this haven. The atmosphere's helped greatly by the friendly staff, particularly Les. So next time the seagulls' shrieking wakes you at an ungodly hour, take a wander and find a special place – *the Market Diner*. Insomnia need not be a problem – use the experience.

The Open Door
by Malcolm Williams

The house in Newhaven to me is a good home with a lot of love in it. With my daughter and two sons and my wife there we shared a lot of good times when I got wed to the girl of my dreams. To live there was heaven. I spent a lot of time working on this house where I was going to share the rest of my life with the ones I love dearly.

The front door as it opened gave me a feeling of being wanted. And at times that door frame seemed to smile at me after a hard day's work.

I still love this house even after my marriage broke up. And I miss my family.

Our Kitchen
by Judith Greenfield

Our kitchen was probably less than ten foot square, but so much happened in there it was like a TARDIS. Early on, there was no fridge – just a box with a wire mesh front in the larder; and in there too on the floor, eggs in a bucket of isinglass. We kept a few chickens. What the cupboards and drawers held was a mystery to me. I can say that the sink was under the window next to the twin tub, but that's all. It was just our main route from the house, either to school or to play in the garden, or round and about the neighbourhood. If she'd just washed the floor there would be stepping stones of newspaper for us to walk over on our way in and out.

It was Mum's workplace and how she produced what she did in

there still fills me with amazement. She worked all week as a teacher, yet every Saturday, come what may, she would prepare from scratch fish and chips for lunch for the whole family and any friends that us three children had round to play. Groceries were delivered from the *Co-op* and the baker, milkman, fishmonger and butcher all called each week.

I can remember Mum singing at the sink, "Oh for the wings of a dove" or, "I'm HAPPY", but I still had to learn about irony back then. She used to jiggle up and down there too because she needed to go to the toilet but wanted to finish what she was doing first.

Muriel
by Josie Darling

My favourite chair is the Parker Knoll chair in my kitchen. Did you know that Parker Knoll is the caviar of chair makers? The chair was bought by my sensible grandmother in her brown lace up shoes and the chair is not beautiful, chic or luxurious. It is a Presbyterian chair, comfortable and high quality, like a nice piece of cheese. As I lean back I can feel its whole respectable nervous system, and its short wooden legs would never wobble. As I sit there I can see all the way up to my front door and I feel like the captain of the ship with my tribe around me; in the bosom of the house with my dog and my drink beside me, I am safe. I used to sit here and breastfeed, while the afternoon sun filled the kitchen with orange light and the radio bubbled away. If this chair had a name it would be Muriel.

An Alabama Home
by Maggs Radcliffe

Cold concrete dressed up in cheap linoleum rose up like the floor of a prison cell greeting my early morning bare feet. Wakey Wakey shock therapy. The bedroom left much to be desired as well. Stark panelled walls with a small austere rectangle cave recessed into them for a closet. No door. Just a mere muslin curtain veiled my wardrobe. An old metal bed, as noisy as tin cans tied on the back of a bride and groom's wedding carriage, parked itself in a corner whilst a tiny pastiche brand dresser, asking to be left alone, was far too musty to coffin my glad rags.

The living room? Well, let's not bother. Visualize an extension of the bedroom with an over stuffed, badly worn and smelly orange covered chair and a gas heater straight out of a Bela Lugosi movie lurking in the corner rather threateningly.

The kitchen was redeeming. A delightful old sink straight out of the 1920s cradled a brilliant fuchsia bougainvillea which fell through the window in full bloom on summer mornings. I had to literally lift it back into its natural surroundings to access the taps for morning coffee.

My Flatmate
by Rob Stride

I have a flatmate called Gilly (Gilbert), a 9-year-old fell terrier. You can smell him before you see him but he has a heart of gold, the rectum of Satan himself, but a heart of gold. He's an old dog that's had a bit of a miserable life. He has the libido of Casanova and the mind of Thora Hird. He's my flatmate but I don't own him because he doesn't give a ****, and if he wants to sneak out and off, he bloody well will, but he always comes back.

He's been my constant companion for quite a few months now, clearing up puke, shit and bile is quite a boring process. Still he doesn't seem to mind doing it. Gilbert has three modes: 1) The Grumpy Old man, 2) The Silly Puppy and 3) Poorly Dog and you never know which one you're getting.

As soon as he's out of the door he rolls in bitch-piss. His favourite body spray. His Lynx Africa.

When I first got him his stomach was much worse than it is at the moment and when he pooed it was in little bits here and there. I used six bags one day and then he did a big wet one outside the college opposite the British Museum. Great, I had an audience and a big sweaty wet poo. Holding Gill's collar I stretched to the bin and pulled out what I thought was an empty bag. As I started to scoop Gill's poo, it became apparent that the bag had already been used for the same thing and this warm mixture was sloshing about in the bag I was using to pick up another sloshy mixture. I gagged for England much to the joy of the large group of Japanese students.

Gill's favourite food is chicken, brown rice and little porridge oats and bit of quinoa flakes. This keeps him regular. I take him busking but if it's sunny he chases my guitar's reflection on the ground. This is a problem because Gill's lead is attached to my boot, which means that halfway through my rendition of Mercedes Benz, Gill's off, and half my body starts break dancing. I'm sure a few tourists believe that I'm having some kind of fit.

Hove
by Bernie O'Donnell

Hove is a staid, boring place, Brighton's next door but straight-laced aunty. You need a zimmer frame to be allowed across the border.

I lived in Deptford, inner London. It was an exciting place. I'd had three burglaries in a year. Exciting.

In my road pay parties could start on a Saturday and continue booming out till Tuesday morning. Exciting.

Water poured from the ceiling of my flat. When I went upstairs the drug dealers swore it wasn't coming from their flat. Sometimes they actually believed it. My girlfriend would beg me not to confront the dealers – you didn't know who you'd meet. Exciting place.

My friend from Hove moved to Australia and wanted me to house sit until his place was sold. It was deadly quiet. No two-day parties. No burglaries. No fights outside drug dealers' dens. The car windows were still there in the morning.

Hove's boring.

Home and Away
by Laila Raphael

Chicken schnitzels, *The Muppet Show*, Carmel market in Tel Aviv, over ripe tomatoes, pomegranates.

I remember the smell and the flies. My Mum loved it. I wanted the tomatoes less ripe, like in England. English tomatoes, slightly under ripe. I loved them in brown bread sandwiches with pepper, after a trip to *Sainsburys*.

I wanted to return to gloomy England with its rain: it suited my mood. But my Mum would cook real chicken schnitzels in Israel – they were delicious; chicken cooked in batter with those wretched over ripe tomatoes.

Why did she cook chicken schnitzels in Israel, and in England it was all roast dinner, Yorkshire pudding, gravy all that? Chicken schnitzels, spaghetti bolognaise and gold star beer for the grown ups; except it was with rice not spaghetti, and I was very annoyed about that.

My Dad would have curry sandwiches every day: the cold curry looked like an omelette. Dad worked nights and before going he would take my brother and I to the kiosk to buy sweets. When we ate lunch, I often watched *The Muppet Show*. We had a flat with a balcony and a view of the sea.

When we went back to England, we never ate chicken schnitzels or spaghetti bolognaise with rice again.

London in the 1970s
by Richard Laidler

Welcome to London of the outlawed and refugee. A city's haze of delirium torched the inky blackness. I ain't going to work on Maggie's farm no more. Corrugated iron boards windows and wind rattles locks. Strangers walk by on stairs with candles. There is an alloy of Patchouli and Nepalese in the air and rock and roll from the subterranean kingdom beneath the floor! Defiance speaks, bears the testimony. "Welcome to Rue Morgue Avenue," written on the door opposite the kitchen. Was it Brecht written on the wall of the Baader Meinhof's decorous home? "Argue with a Molotov".

Fifty pence meter in bathroom. No rent books.

"How much social security you get?"

Listen: laughter and TV behind garish wallpaper. Pygmy hand basin, homogenised corridors.

"The last tenant here hung himself by the light bulb."

"Just upped and left, poster, stereo, left it all, he's done it before."

"Pure Zen, really the heart of Kanzeon."

Removal finished at two in the morning: circumstances colloquially known as "moonlighting". Cathedral silence I could not help but feel. Inviolate aura, intangible, but real. People's dwellings take on the characteristics of their owners. You can feel the gloom or lack of warmth. How infrequently it's possible to ruminate that there's been real happiness. Incense like the smell of hashish mingles, unimaginative décor banish thoughts of pathos. Tomorrow is new. Love thy neighbour but I was never taught how.

I heard the busker.

"In our winter's City, one more forgotten hero and a world that doesn't care. Memory fading with the metal ribbons that he wears."

Stark images borne of alienation and homelessness stirred in my awareness. The memories arose and I jotted down the stream.

Unforgiven was at the cinema: the haunted figure riding out of that rain soaked prairie town. I saw that a show about Lenny Bruce was at the theatre and I'd wished I'd alighted spontaneously from the bus to see it. He'd held a mirror to the neuroses and taboos of the early sixties. I was not in the West End any more but the same street. Like the myths and legends surrounding the luminaries and icons of past time it was hard to believe my story was true.

"That house is gone," shouted the builder as I walked past.

"You ought to see this place he's living in," a friend had remarked.

"You're not English, are you?" The Community Stores had directed me to some address that might be helpful.

I thought home was an Ex Prime Minister until I discovered Camden Town: the reference on the chalk marked wall was to Alexander Douglas Home.

Homes due to be demolished, but with the amenities still functional, had been taken over to fill the dire need. I never knew that such a place could exist, wrought out of the desperation of the homeless. It was my first encounter with Student Community Housing.

Sooner than anticipated, with a modicum of prior notice, just a brief explanation, all would be gone. All ultimately soon to be nothing more than rubble and debris. It was as if in these drastic circumstances there was nothing left to cling to and it was mirrored in the environment. The breakdown of mediocrity had caused dissatisfaction with the conventional idea of home. By nightfall it might be gone and the ephemeral quality had penetrated the moment.

In night time London I saw a placard about asylum. Everywhere on the subway posters proclaimed the message of asylum. White posters on walls were indicating Asylum was near. I'd reflected it must be the other, the they or somebody else. But then the advance notice for the movie changes: Asylum is waiting for you. When I'd opened a door to the vagabond looking for shelter it was as if I'd been struck by a heavy weight. Filthy clothes, smell of cider, bruises and a huge stomach showed the hard road travelled.

"You could stay in our basement but I wouldn't recommend it, it's a bit cold and windy."

"I need somewhere to have a baby."

I'd experienced the Orwellian soup kitchen and the public baths. I'd gone into the disused past accidentally: I was one more of the left be-hinds.

"Hey, Jimmy! Hey, pal. I'll see you Jimmy."

The saddest thing is an outsider among outsiders.

Sheltered with the anaesthetising bottle of 'Jack' were the meth drinkers. Huddled against the alien world, they laughed and shouted at the wicked world beyond the circle surrounding the fire on no man's land. You can leave here for awhile, company's a silver needle, sweats, cramps and hallucinations. If you let go of the world, who to judge, who to blame? Home's the cold shoulder of society.

I had been in London just a short time and experienced things I never knew could possibly have existed: wanderers looking for shelter, takeo-ver bids for rooms, baths in rusty tubs, dubious elements in the police and a living space looking like a deleted scene from Easy Rider, to list some!

On the walls of Ladbroke Grove kids' school was scrawled in huge black capitals: We teach old hearts to break. Mandela's, Luther King's and Ghandi's weren't exactly wanted.

I'd often hear Cat Stevens as I made my way and my home. The Incredible String Band on auto would not allow a neighbour to sleep. Take me to lands distant and fair: all night long. A friend stayed in a 'tuppenny lean' that had been there since Victorian times. After a night of alcohol you pay a small sum to be leant over, if you're strung out for somewhere to stay...

A neighbour had climbed onto the roof, climbing through the skylight with his flute, in the distance somebody else had the same idea with a guitar. I never did believe one of the visitors had jammed with Hendrix at the Isle of Wight.

I'd heard a song as I'd arrived home, exuding and emanating through the doors. It had been about a shop's doorway revealing the chimes of freedom. Numerous recollections and reflections, included the refugee on the unarmed road of flight. The fusion of the wedding bells and the wild ripping hail. I felt every movement of the composition: the clanging, jolting, precipitating of church bells tolling and the mad mystic hammering. I could hear it so clearly, happening for the guardians and protectors of the mind and the poet and painter far behind their rightful time. All while avoiding the saturation downpour.

My story of a space I'd rather have forgotten about occupied my consciousness. My ragged edge existence arose in definition. A capacity to recall had been accessed and the futility of what the private landlord has to offer had been the catalyst.

"You're not one of these poster on the wall people, are you?"

"No, I'm a cut above the average tenant."

'All property is theft' was the last of the radical artwork to catch my attention as I left the street with one last turnaround: Karl Marx and his unspiritual ideology.

"So far away, doesn't anybody stay in one place anymore," the café's radio said. It filled me with an eerie sense to realise it was gone. All vanished with the times which are never to return. It's enough to make you sad, the deserted remains.

There's no one home and al have moved on. The labyrinth of streets razed to the ground, the children whom no longer played in the same streets. Was it only yesterday angry slogans adorned ascending murals, welcome doors and sunrise windows, now rainbow dream walls creak in protest and the whole street is empty. Familiar rooms that once were sonorous with the sound of acoustic guitar, perhaps resonant with laughter, were just a drone, a distant hum of workmen's machinery.

A part of me too had arisen and passed on forever, reminding me of the lonesome hobo confronting me so unavoidably on the frozen morning. Far into the distance the bulldozers roared, just the whirlwind of frenetic activity that was London remained. It was just memories that were to greet my thoughts, poignant ones. The Greater London Council's decision had been adamant and the action aligned with the difficulty had taken place. Petitions had been shredded into insignificance.

A licence to destroy had been endorsed by yet one more petty official.

Appearances Can Be Deceptive
by Candida Ford

The chair had a cottage type appearance and looked really inviting especially after a hard day's work; really pretty, with lovely plump cushions that looked as though one could curl up on it with a cat. I sat down heavily and went straight through because most of the straps across the base had broken and the cushions had just been placed over the top for the sake of appearances.

My legs were sticking straight up in the air and in a panic to save myself I grabbed the arms which were weakened with age and wood-worm. They broke off in my hands.

Here I Rest
by Gordon Radcliffe

THE Chair, so much more than a seat, is the socket from which I can draw the energy that empowers me. Ekorne, in tan brown soft leather, a recliner with a matching footstool, is comfort to the point of indulgent sloth. Set out in front is the computer monitor, DVD, broadband Internet, media centre operating system, integrated TV tuner, and instant access to a life-record of photo images and music.

It backs onto the bookcase holding a broad collection of ready-reference favourites. To the right a mounted, back illuminated, stained glass window of St George stands permanent guard. Pensioned off from some unremembered Gothic pile, lost years, till we met in an antique shop in Islington.

To the left a sliding glass door presents a panoramic southern view across an expansive opening of the bay. The water's reliable glitter, in the reflected sunlight, is replaced at night by the blinking red and green lights of the channel navigation markers. In the mid distance jetties, docks, boats ceaselessly bustle. Here I relax, no unfulfilled ambition. I have arrived; here I rest.

Ticket to Ride

butlins
by Anthony Spiers

we do ride a steamer train. it stops into some buffers at butlins holiday camp in clacton on top of the sea. we have to go inside a long factory place. light blue paint and white paint on the colour the sky gets when the weather is a nice day. I see toy soldiers growing right up to the roof with red cheeks on and busby hats. we get our keys and pin ourselves with our badges and look for our own chalet to have our holiday in.

a chalet word means this sort of shed. bed bunks going on top of the other one like red buses with the upstairs. I bagsy the top or billy might fall off. I like sleeping high up the treetops way like owl birds. billy has bad skins in his toes. it goes dropping off the way skins on onions and brown ointment to put on in a little wooden tub. here's our trunk big box of sometimes treasure inside it's just our holiday clothes. they go all squashed away small with a stuffy trunky smell. not a dumbo elephant trunk michael says I'm dumbo because my ears poke out I was a baby and they pushed them down with sticky plasters.

LADS and LASSES means the toilets are in here the letters look almost the same letters. I'm going in the LADS undo my shorts at the front when I'm being excused. their name is called flies not nasty buzzing flies to stick to a flypaper they're only buttons. men can do the echo whistling there because when I whistle my lips they won't do tunes just windy noise.

we play putting it's a sort of golf game with grass. you must knock it a titchy bit into a hole. and a house that jack built the floors and walls all going wonky and a funfair. on the ghost train it keeps bashing through doors and darkness and screeching with skeletons trying to bang into us and the bumper cars with sparks coming out. now we spend a nice quiet ride on the bicycle with four wheels. two people sit back like the kings and peddle our legs round. that's what the daisy daisy song is singing about.

we do wet our whistles in the café. daddy doesn't pick tea because he likes camp coffee juice inside a bottle and a scotchman picture having a kilt because he's scotch in bits. he hasn't got any kilts he wears trousers on his legs but he can play with bagpipes. mummy has a tea drink she's wearing her skirt it goes black one way and yellow along the other way like kilts.

billy and me have brown fizzy cola with a straw you mustn't get a dent in your straw or it won't go sucking ever again. I can swallowing the bubbles up my nose a bit prickly. bubbles hide in the bottle if the lid comes off a big lots of them all try to get out at the same time swimming fast up to the top for air boiling and dizzy. I can make my ear go close. I do hear the bubbles which they sizzle like a quiet sausage.

some redcoats are making men do their nobbly knees competition with their trousers rolling up. laughing up their faces and ladies do the prettiest old granny in the whole world. redcoats have happy red colour blazers on and white colour trousers and white frocks. a big voice called a tannoy follows us about like dogs can and wakes us up for the morning.

we're peckish and at dinnertime it's a giant room with tables and hundreds of tablecloths. our soup is called the windsor brown kind with rolls. I have to tip my bowl up and suck the soup off special spoons like people with table manners and not get it all down me. we eat chickens and funny potatoes and a pink pudding made from ice and wait for our dinner to go down or catch indigestion and have eno's liver salts.

before bedtime we do drink a horlicks drink. the café lady does it in an electric stirring machine with its own foam. in bed I can listen to some voices having a walk outside and shoes to go past our chalet without any people inside them. horlicks is a sleepy white drink of milk made from freshly cows to have sweet sorts of dreams not ghosts or tigers in. black and white cows in fur like countries in a map might go in my dream to eat up their cuds and chew it properly until it makes into the milk. the cows are moving their faces to watch at me with friendly faces on. they don't know how to smile. and don't know how to go to the seaside and do paddling with their feet inside some waves. or catch out some crabs whoppers on a bit of string in the rock pools and how to do screaming on the big dipper and what all the names of ice creams is or dig up a wall with sand to stop the sea splashing over just know everything about the milk.

Nature at Work
by Shelley

The sun was as hot as an oven, baking my skin and lighting the way in Northern Australia, Adelaide River, a beautiful part of the country where crocodiles, frill necked lizards and kangaroos are abundant. I was on the phone, organising and booking accommodation for the 14 or more passengers on the three-day trip from Alice-Springs to Darwin. I was a tour guide/cook; a fantastic job - full of adventure, fun and laughs. One of the pax (passengers) approached and asked me about a snake they had just seen eating a bird. They wanted to know if it was a pet!

"Oh no," I replied. "It's definitely not. Let's go and take a look."

It turned out to be a non-venomous olive python which had recently crushed its victim, a galah – a type of parrot, grey in colour, with a pink frill on its head. We stood looking at this 6ft snake with its mouth fully extended round the galah's head – ready to engulf it. This, as you can imagine, takes some time to do. So – instead of preparing lunch for the group, we all unanimously decided to watch the nature show. The snake slowly manoeuvred the bird down its mouth until it came to the wings which were hoisted up by its sides – so it cleverly regurgitated it a little, coiled some of its body up over the wings and pushed them flat, allowing it to continue to swallow the bird. This took around 20 minutes from beginning to end. When it had consumed the body, it yawned, re-engaging its jaw. We all stood back and it just slid away.

Studland Beach
by Julian Harvey

My Dad was in a foul mood after leaving his keys at the Guest House. Brother Pat dropped his sandwiches in the sand. Smash went the plate over his head. I was amazed at the quickness of my father's temper.

Born Again
by Joe Sheerin

I came to London in the Fifties as a teenager from the rural West of Ireland. It is difficult to explain to anyone who hadn't experienced something similar, just how traumatic an event like that can be. On the day I left home I saw my first train, at Carrick-on-Shannon station. I had seen pictures of trains in books and it was very much as I expected it to look, except that it was bigger and much less glamorous. The carriages were like enclosed cattle trucks. On the same day I saw my first city, which was Dublin. It was the focal point of the map of Ireland on our school wall and all pupils by the age of seven were expected to be able to point it out. The clever ones might be able to show Cork and Galway, even Belfast as well. By the time we reached Dublin it was drawing in the evening and a light, persistent rain was coming down. So many houses and all looking the same. How, in feck's name, could one ever find one's own house out there in that darkening valley of houses upon houses?

At Dun Laoghaire I saw my first boat. It glinted harshly in the wet light. It was as cold as iron and there were cattle on the lower deck, heading ironically for English slaughterhouses. I saw my first black man when the train stopped at Crewe station. I had seen one, a stage Negro, in a film when a travelling cinema came to our village. My uncle, who had never seen a black person in his life, told me 'They're completely different to us in every way entirely'. The train moved off before I could check the veracity of his pronouncement.

At Euston I encountered my first underground experience. I knew about undergrounds but had no idea what to expect. I went up escalators and down escalators and through underground corridors and along platforms and up steps and down steps before, thanks to the kindness of strangers, I was put on the train to Archway. Every time the train started I fell over and whenever the train stopped I danced in the corridor. That underground logo is forever branded on my skull as is the stink of stale air and strangeness of everything. I heard my first foreign language when a group of very dark-haired, dangerous-looking people got on at Camden Town station. I reckon now that they were Greek Cypriots. Because they stood near me I said hello to them and asked them how they were. Luckily they didn't understand my accent and probably decided I was mad.

On the Holloway Road I saw my first trolleybus. I thought it was a fire engine and that the poles were the ladders for the firemen to climb. I saw my first traffic lights at Archway. For no particular reason I stood watching them change from green to red to amber to green to red to amber to green. I saw my first block of flats along St John's Way. They were only four storeys high but they impressed me so much that I sat on the garden wall of the house opposite them and looked and looked. I saw too my first woman who seemed like a film star.

Everywhere everybody seemed to be in such a feckin' hurry. They ran or they pushed you out of the way or they glared at you for stopping. In Ireland the only time we ever ran was when somebody was dying and we ran for the priest, or when a cow fell over the edge and we ran to get help to pull her out before she slipped to her death, or on a beautiful early sunny morning in summer when it was so breathtaking that you ran across the river meadows for the pure joy of it. Over a twenty-four hour spell my eyes and my nose and my ears were been reprogrammed and my brain was trying to make sense of it all. I didn't realise it at the time but it would take years to complete.

It is said that if a first offender were sentenced to one day in prison and then released he would never re-offend. So it is with the emigrant. Later that day in my room I sat chain smoking Woodbines and feeling very confused. I really needed somebody to talk to, somebody who was in the same boat as myself. Together we might make some sense of it. I pretended to look out the window but instead I was longing for the odour of dung, the sound of horses and the sight of white mist moving down the purple of Slieve an Iarann. If I could have gone back at that moment and saved face then I would have. And lived forever afterwards on the experience.

I think the only other experience similar to being an arriving immigrant is being born. This occurred to me when I saw my son coming into this bloody world. After some long hours of struggle he slid suddenly and in a great hurry into an angular and whitewashed ward in Newmarket Maternity Hospital. He gasped and then screamed in terror. "That's a good sign," said the midwife reassuringly, "he'll be a talker.'" It would take up to ten good years for my son to learn the language of that room. In the meantime he would have to well and truly forget the secret language of the womb.

Even if your language is English there are literally hundreds of new concrete nouns, hundreds of variations of nuance and tone in adjectives and adverbs, many hundreds of new idioms and structures. And then there is the accent. And you had better learn their language. Because, as sure as cheese, they won't be bothering to learn yours.

Despite all that, the majority of us who set out on the journey, do arrive. On the way we are often seen as stupid because we confuse the doctor with the nurse, or seen as taciturn and sullen when we refuse to identify the midwife, because we might get it wrong. On the positive side, though, many of us are lucky enough to meet one or two people who understand us and accept us as we are. One of these we marry. The other becomes our lover. Or whatever.

Letter from Laos
by Jaelithe Casteel

Dear Greg and Nick,

I hope you're both well. At the moment I'm sitting in a narrow boat slicing its way up the Mekong River in Laos. Sun's beating down, engine's hot and noisy, breathtaking views of the forests on the hills, and grey and black mountains striated with red and white. We pass bamboo-house villages on the banks, set on stilts up the hillside. Kids wave as we go past, happy to communicate with human beings from outside their village limits, even for a general wave directed at the whole crowd. I love picking out one kid – one always stands out – our eyes meet, we both wave tentatively. Within a couple of seconds, both waves are firmer, more self-assured, confident in the continued response. A fleeting relationship is established between two human beings with unknown backgrounds, but definitely from different worlds, unimaginable to each other. Their enthusiasm infected me at the beginning of our journey upriver. These were precious moments: a closeness across the water, an understanding of the joy of living, the importance of being acknowledged, the here and now.

A sadness comes over me every time the boat takes me mercilessly onwards, out of sight, away from a young life with unlimited possibilities and twists, but only one realisable path. What will it be? What will mine be? Both of us will probably never know each other's destiny, but our lives touched for a few precious moments.

Water buffaloes lie submerged along the banks in groups, their heads sticking out, wide muzzles with large rounded nostrils snorting and waggling their ears to keep the flies away. Same as the children, they follow our progress, turning their heads in unison. However, I don't feel any kinship with these life forms, can't begin to imagine what's going on behind those bulbous eyes. We just happen to be at the same place at the same time. Rhetorical watching, no understanding.

On this trip I'm realising my place on this planet, as an exploring homo sapiens caucasian, searching for a mate and fulfilment of my own potential, my dreams becoming more defined and therefore closer to my reach. For a while, running with three others of the same breed: still each of us separated by our genes and the experiences that are filtered through our personalities and built up by up-bringing.

I'm wandering around Laos. Possible relationships are encountered but highly improbable due to different lifestyles and aspirations and simple geographical location. They are set in an infrastructure built from tradition and touched by communism; contained in a beautiful, natural environment. To me, the biggest crime would be to destroy this nature or let it be destroyed.

At the rapids I wonder if we'll make it back alive.

Love Jaelithe

Death in Barcelona
by Laila Raphael

I was there when they pulled you to the ground.

One of us was gone. God knows what made me turn round; it's a long time ago. We had spent the day at the fiesta, a group of us all going our separate ways, and we were walking along beside the floats, laughing, happy, dancing, light.

I turned around and saw you disappearing, sinking into a hazy circle of youths, like a rag doll falling into quick sand. It was a moment where the movie changed into something else, but none of us comprehended what the image in front of us really meant. My friend Sarah was the first to realise what was happening, as she was nearer. Time became distorted as you ran literally for your life. We followed you and found you face down in a pool of blood in the darkened road like a shadow outlined in paint, surrounded by a small crowd, again circling your defeated body.

We went into the ambulance in a state of shock; that feeling you get when your head is concussed and you're almost slightly high and can't quite feel yet. You died in hospital, knife wound to the femoral artery. The irony is if you had not run you might have lived.

I hardly knew you. Sarah knew you better: a strange man, intelligent, a scientist, a spiritual seeker like us. The papers reported the next day that there had not been much trouble this year, only one death. Sarah and I stayed together for days finding comfort in each other's company.

Apparently, you had been depressed at times, and had discussed suicide to a friend of ours, and what you would have used was a knife. You had maybe wound some young men up in a bar with something you said, the wrong look, the wrong vibration. We wondered if you had chosen it, if your soul had decided to go, but this is a big question and all I know was that I was deeply affected and scared. I had seen death before but this was different. Sarah was frightened, as she was told by the police that being the closest, they would like her to give evidence. I was spooked and wanted to leave Barcelona.

They caught them eventually. I fled too.

Elephant Trekking
by Jaelithe Casteel

During my stay in southern Thailand near Krabi, I went on *Nosey Parker's Elephant Trek*. What an amazing experience, trekking through the jungle on an elephant's back, lulled in a steady slow motion. Well worth the 750 Baht (11 pounds sterling).

The shuttle bus picked me up bang on time and took us five tourists seven kilometres through the countryside to the elephant camp. When I got out of the bus, a four-metre high beast clocked me and moved in my direction, its massive long trunk extended towards me. I absolutely shat myself and moved backwards, him coming ever forward. I didn't know whether looking steadily in his tiny eye would be good or bad, so in the end I turned my back and quickly stepped away.

Two questions in my mind: how were we expected to climb up there? More importantly, was this a good idea? A girl showed us to a bamboo hut on stilts, that was the way up. I was paired with a Thai girl, and they told me she'd never been on an elephant before either. To get on the two-seater saddle, you have to step on the neck but I was scared of hurting the animal, and unsteady through adrenaline pumping. Finally I managed it, still not knowing what I was in for.

I was scared of falling off, and the elephant man thought it was funny to pretend to grab me and the Thai girl by the ankle to pull us off. We had to cross a stream, the elephant leaning forward and us two girls holding on for dear life. The elephant's name is Song-Laa, the elephant man told me. He is the "mahout", training the elephant and staying with it as its master for most of its life.

It's amazing how they pick their way over and around rocks, even though they have such tiny eyes. I don't know about memory, but elephants certainly have a lot of patience, moving slowly but steadily.

Gradually we relax and I start to enjoy the trek, the elephants grabbing leaves along the way and eating. Then our mahout decides it's photo time, takes my camera and gets off his beast. Straightaway the elephant moves sideways and turns, us girls nearly screaming with fear. The guy just moves into a better position to take photos, me wishing he'd get back on his animal and, please, not lose my camera lens cover. He takes it all in his stride. Three photos and he remounts. We feel visibly better.

The trail takes us through the rubber plantation. Monkeys leap in the branches. The rubber trees are striated with a knife, and a bucket collects the rubber. The guide tells us they sell it to Michelin afterwards. I can smell the rubber; the first time I've seen where it comes from.

After another scary ride down and uphill, the five elephants stop together: it's another photo session. The elephant man slips off his mount. This time he wants me to sit on the elephant's neck for the picture. I don't really want to get off my perch: it looks dangerous, but I can't chicken out in front of everyone. I ungracefully slip onto his neck and my Thai friend holds onto me: she's scared too. The animal starts flapping its ears - not too hard - but its hairs are stiff and spiky and prick my legs, it hurts! The guy's not satisfied with one photo; I have to bear it longer.

On the way back to the camp, I wonder at how these huge beasts let themselves be dominated by Man. The mahouts have ice-picks on sticks, which they use gently now and then. That's on fully-grown animals, but how much hitting goes into training a young elephant? Later I saw a mahout fully beat one of the elephants several times and bring him back to be chained up. Maybe it was misbehaving. It was horrible to see.

At camp, we feed the elephants small cucumbers provided, and take more photos. They really are formidable to behold from the ground. The guide takes us to watch the elephants bathe, including a three-year old baby. It's cute, but whenever the baby tries to climb onto the bank a guy hits it with the ice-pick. Makes me sick. In the leaflet it said to consider the reputation of an elephant camp, as a number of operators seriously abuse the elephants and/or fail to provide adequate shade and water for their well being.' They had a licence number too. If this is good care, I dread to think what other elephants' conditions are like.

Resting Place (Uluru)
by Shelley

Ghost gums silhouetted in the haze of dawn,
terracotta coloured sand underfoot, the sky stretching blue,
flies awaken in a squadron, military fashion,
breath is heavy, heart palpitating, and the mouth dry.
A monumental resting place – initiations of young men.
Magnificent energy absorbed within
the extreme intense heat scorching skin
respect – reflect.

Photographs and Memories

I've Seen the Pictures
by Michelle Brown

I've seen the pictures of my Mum before I was born.

I see her young and fun loving with her ironed-straight hair and her flares and her micro minies, her long, long endless legs looking too fragile to support her, like a foal's. The first flush of romance with my Dad, opposites attract, him a bit of an acid casualty with bushy hair and a slightly silly Jesus beard, which for some reason he combed into two prongs.

Their wedding day, alight with happiness, the two distinct tribes, my Dad's stuffy middle class army stock, my Mum's poorer working class, descended from gypsies and her brother the result of a wartime fling with an American Indian GI, who had grown up eating bread and dripping, with sheep's brains on toast as a treat on Sundays.

Walking Across the Ouse
by David Boxall

I was there when one could have walked across the River Ouse. Every type of ship, boat, landing craft you could imagine was there. Not a channel of water between them. They extended way up beyond the old swing bridge, down to the river's mouth. Seaford Bay was reserved for the big stuff.

I was walking to school that day and shall never forget those words.

"Why, you could walk across anywhere without using the bridge",

Yet I don't remember any people. But, what was even more unbelievable, the very next morning at the same spot at the same time, I looked down on the river and saw nothing. Well, nothing but the river. Overnight every craft must have been moved without a sound.

D-day had started.

Photo at Hanging Rock
by Dee Hesling

I don't remember the day the photo was taken, all of us sitting in a circle in our Sunday best. We jokingly call it "Picnic at Hanging Rock".

It's the one common denominator that bonds our respective homes. Mine is on the pine dresser, sister Monica's on her bookshelf, brother in Cork has his in the hall in a little enclave window, sister in Australia has hers in the downstairs loo.

We all stare out at the camera: Mother, Father leaning on the straw bale, me age six with a melting bar of chocolate in my hand, held like an ice lolly about to be licked - brothers leaning on each other playfully.

I look at it and try to remember the dress. Where did I get it? The big starched bow...

Future Tense
by A.K. Andrew

Past, present and future may seem a logical progression, except I might be getting stuck on that last part: it looks as if I have secondary breast cancer. At least that's the current thought on the preliminary findings. I'll know for sure when I get my results on Wednesday. Last summer, when they took away my right breast, I was upset and felt a sense of loss. Now, I can barely see why I was so upset over one breast. It wasn't even a large breast, barely a B-cup. Nothing compared to a whole future. It's ironical really, as in recent years the future is what I've had a propensity to live in. You know the kind of thing – Oh, things will be better after I've had a vacation, when I've moved, when I have a different job etc. Try as I might, I have found that staying in the present has been hard. Now I don't want to leave it, reluctant to go any further.

It's one o'clock in the morning, I can't sleep and I don't want to think about any of that. So I let my mind wander into the past, where at least I have control over where I go. Tonight I choose to go to a place where I went before I became overburdened by responsibilities: twenty five years ago when I first arrived in San Francisco from London, and was desperately looking for work. It's fun to laugh at myself over the myriad of things I did and just how naïve I was. Leaving England at twenty-eight, I thought I'd learned some street smarts from being in London for five years. What a joke! Talk about green and Fresh Off the Boat...It was like I'd leapt back in age to my early twenties. Appropriate actually, as I was ripe for new experiences and ready to let go of the blinkered self-obsession of 70s lesbian feminism.

Someone told me that you could make a lot of money busking. Maybe you can, but somehow the financial district lunchtime crowd were not wowed by the folksy, early skiffle stuff I was giving them. After two hours, there was $1.50 in my guitar case. Someone else told me that waiting tables paid well, so I went round a bunch of restaurants asking if anyone was hiring. Of course the slight flaw in that plan was when asked if I had any experience, I said no. Duh! Hey FOB, catch clue. I even went into McDonalds and was turned down. Figuring that was pretty low, I gave up for the day.

Then I decided to try my hand, so to speak, at one of the massage parlours. Now, I didn't really know what went on in them, but I did know it was more than just a normal massage. How bad could it be though, I thought? After all they are legal aren't they? So I took my nervous, middleclass self down to the Tenderloin, walking past the hookers, junkies, transvestites and the homeless, my natural blond hair shining out like a beacon. I decide to brave 'Les Nuits de Paris'. A bell announced my arrival and I entered a small "inviting" entrance lobby with red and purple velvet draped walls. A couple of rather bored looking, heavily made-up women were sitting around. Both were wearing extremely short, black satin hot pants, black fishnets and low-cut white satin tops. Whatever I was wearing certainly didn't scream back under wear. Not even a trace of mascara on my face. They shot a glance at each other, then at me. One of them, very friendly like said,

"Can I help you?"

Me trying to act casual about looking for work prompted one of them to get the manager. A few minutes later, a rather seedy looking guy in a rather tired looking suit, appeared from behind one of the curtains. Looking me up and down, he asked in a slow, slimy voice if I'd had any experience. Again I said no. Would I like to fill in an application form? Well, miss Fresh Off the Boat filled it in with the truth: College, Primary School Teacher and Community Arts! For goodness sake – who goes for a job at a massage parlour and earnestly puts down that they used to take kids on photography trips? Of course he took one look at it and said he'd be in touch if they were hiring. After I left, thoroughly mortified by the whole experience, I imagined them all rolling their eyes, laughing at my naiveté.

A couple of weeks later I finally landed a job dishwashing and bussing tables at a dessert café up on Haight St. called 'Kiss my Sweet'.

It was great, my first job in America, a new immigrant starting on the bottom rung doing something I would never have dreamt of doing in security blanketed, dole clad England. Haight Ashbury was still pretty cool, filled with a bunch of freaks and weirdoes: aging hippies who had never left, sixteen year old ones who were just getting started, all thrown in with street hustlers, punks, artists and queers. I felt like I was coming home, more alive than I'd ever been, really living for the moment. I actually liked the work and the other staff were cool: people from all over, no one actually born in San Francisco. I later had friends who were from San Francisco, but probably 85% of the population come from somewhere else. Which meant that they were almost all there out of choice. Very different from a 1981 London where everyone I knew was desperate to leave. San Francisco was such a beautiful city. Fresh, clean air, clear sunny days, temperate weather, and rows of decoratively detailed Victorian pastel painted houses, hills with views to die for. In the late afternoon a fog rolled off the Pacific Ocean over the Golden Gate Bridge, cloaking the city in mystery and romance. I had landed in paradise.

$3.75 an hour part-time wasn't really going to pay the rent though, so I fairly quickly went through a series of interim jobs including being a house painter and working downtown as a receptionist. I was fired from that one as apparently the customers had complained that they couldn't understand my English accent! I guess it was ok to suffer the humiliation of being fired at least once in my life. The best short-term job I had was being a transport surveyor, which basically meant sitting on various buses with a clicker counting the number of people getting on. The exciting part was doing the same thing on the Cable Cars: the grip man constantly burning up the brakes on the incredibly steep hills, forever ringing the bell, hoping the cable wouldn't break and people hanging off the side trying not to get decapitated by a Cable Car coming the other way.

Finally I got a real job and became a seamstress at 'A Taste of Leather', one of the gay men's leather shops South of Market. Now, by that I mean an SM leather store, selling adult toys, leather restraints and everything you'd need for any bondage scenario. This was pretty new to a fun environment and generally me. Not only did I get to make sex toys all day, the head cashier was a very cute lesbian. She had a very fluffy, blonde girlfriend who worked as an erotic dancer at the Lusty Lady, a woman owned burlesque/strip club. (It actually unionised in the late 90's). My eyes were opened to a positive new perspective of women who actually chose to work in the sex industry. I was well and truly on board.

By fall, I had moved up another rung of the immigrant ladder to work at 'Image Leather'. This was a more upscale leather store by way of being in the Castro, which had become a fashionable neighbourhood and the heart of the gay community in the city. That's where I really learned how to work with leather, teasing the suppleness through the sewing-machine, the smoothness between my hands a pleasure to work with. Every mistake showed as the needle punctured the shiny surface, which was a little nerve-wracking given the expense, but it merely heightened the thrill of the learning curve. The pungent smell was so intense that it was even noticeable walking by the outside of the store. Best of all I really loved my new gay male friends. I was the only woman, but that suited me. Kerry was the head tailor, and he and I immediately had a great rapport.

Rapport? Who are you calling a whore? He would have quipped.

We shared an "easily amused" sense of humour and just cracked up all day. He'd do silly things like loop the leather thongs attached to the end of black leather dildos, over his ears, swinging them from side to side like two giant pendulous earrings. Then there was Frank, who was drop dead gorgeous - lots of long lunches for Frank! Another guy, named Lopaka, boasted of having sex with a different guy every night for the last 9 months. He was unable to see that maybe there was a reason no one wanted a repeat performance. The phrase Safe Sex had not yet been coined, let alone used. Meanwhile the owner was a major lush and an object of our derision. He would euphemistically "go to the bank" every day around 10.30 a.m. returning around 3.p.m, totally wasted. Then he'd go to the back room either with some young boy in tow, or just to sleep it off.

While the bitchiness was mostly good humoured, there was definite-ly no room for being thin-skinned. One of the guys coming in looking the worse for wear would evoke a barrage of comments:

"Oooh girlfriend! - Look what the cat's dragged in."

"Don't you mean butt-dragged?"

"Guess someone had her bell rung last night."

"Wonder what side of whose bed she got out of this morning."

"Side of the gutter more like".

Naturally the main topic was sex, and there was certainly no shortage of material for discussion it seemed.

"Wouldn't mind the UPS guy handle my package with care".

"University? Yes I went to the Sorebunne"

You get the picture. Frank himself could have kept us all going, with a combination of suave charm, mixed with a devilish sense of humour. It was kind of frustrating too though being round all this sex stuff all day as I had a major crush on a woman who I had fooled around with one Sunday afternoon in August, but who was then playing hard to get.

For four months in fact. As I left on Christmas Eve, Frank, with his usual salacious sparkle, told me he hoped I got what I wanted for Christmas. I knew exactly what that was.

I can see her so clearly in my minds eye standing in the bar that night: short, dark brown hair, kind of slicked back, bright red 50's open neck twill shirt, sleeves rolled up slightly from her wrists, her long legs in a pair of 501's. One of her black cowboy boots was propped back against the pillar she was leaning on next to the pool table. She was so goddamn hot. We'd been hanging and playing pool all evening, but now it was late and the bar would be closing soon. So after I took my shot, I went up to her, my arms circling her waist and she pulled me towards her and kissed me. We spent that night in her bed, just sleeping, but the next day I got exactly what I had wanted for Christmas. That was 25th December 1982.

It must be nearly five o'clock now, as I have just heard the milkman driving his milk float down the road. When I moved back here a few years ago I couldn't believe how ubiquitous they were; like a lost relic from a bygone England. The soft snoring of my girlfriend asleep beside me washes over and comforts me in its gentle rhythm. It means it is still the present and I am still here with her. She occasionally wears that red shirt now and again, the cowboy boots not so much. Her dark brown hair is flecked with silver at the sides and now she wears little round metal glasses when she reads a book, which I think are sexy as hell.

At some point in the future I could tell you a lot more about my past. When I get my results on Wednesday, I'll find out if I have the time.

Fame
by Yvonne Luna

I was there when Pete Townsend smashed his guitar into the stage. I thought it was my fault. I was standing in the front row with Anna wearing my top hat so I stuck out of the crowd. And there was that moment, where Pete saw me. He looked straight at me, pointed at my hat and did a 'nice one' sign with his thumb, smiling. But I froze. I stopped cheering and dancing and froze to the spot. I must have looked absolutely horrified and affronted. And that was when he did it. Looked embarrassed, put out, lifted his guitar right up into the air, right over his head, and SMASH - down it came - yes, as I said, all my fault, because I

DIDN'T SMILE BACK. I didn't know then that he was wont to do this kind of thing on a regular basis.

And I'm still just as bad. Get completely star struck, like fame belongs to some Godlike creatures and that we have no right to even look at them unless we've paid to. I suppose, generally speaking, it doesn't matter. But I went out with a poet who, when I first knew him, was no more famous than me. He'd been mentioned in Melody Maker once when he sang for the punk outfit 'The Cat Wax Axe Company', but that was it. I could handle that. But then he got to be with me, and I guess I got to give him lots of confidence, me being so great and all that, and telling him what a God and what a genius he was the whole time. Well, I must be very good with words because he believed me. In fact, every-one was starting to believe he was a Poetry God, and next I knew he was up there supporting Nick Cave at his book readings, hanging out with George Melly, getting invited here, there and everywhere. And we both got given gold passes to all the coolest clubs meaning we could just go in for free. But when the phone rang, it was always for him. And when we were out together, everyone wanted to talk to him, offer him the gigs, him the book deals. Hey, hey! I'm a poet too. Look, here's one I did … Women threw themselves at him, one was even naked when she opened her door to him when he 'popped round to talk about an interview'.

Shit, I hate fame. It's like Death. I couldn't handle the jealousy or the worry. I lost all confidence in myself. We split up. And suddenly the gold cards didn't work any more.

The Photograph Album
by Josephine

"Jo, let's have a nice smile. I'm sure you can do better than that!" My face is set with eyes screwed up against the sun and, even if I can, there is no way I am going to smile at the photographer sent by the local newspaper.

The photo captures more than two scowling siblings standing in a field that sunny July morning in 1970. We are bookends to our mother Deborah who – at 26 – is still beautiful but fearful that raising two children on her own means that her one major asset is fading fast. Despite the fact that the so called swinging sixties has just given way to the liberated seventies, attractive divorced mothers are a threat to the way of life in this sleepy seaside community.

Deborah dominates the scene. She smiles directly into the camera with her hands on her hips which are barely covered with turquoise hot pants. Deborah has good legs and natural long blond hair topped up with a bottle as the golden shine had started to diminish over the years. Either side her children are dressed almost identically in blue trousers with turn ups, white shirts and black shiny shoes. One is a cuddly five-year-old with piles of short blond curls and a sullen face; his usual sunny smile deserting him today. The other is me, an eight year old, and in contrast to my brother I am skinny with long red hair. I've got bored of being labelled the quiet, clever one as well as permanently irritated by the number of adults who tell me to "Cheer up, it may never happen!" I wanted to tell them that it already has…

Despite our many differences and constant bickering my brother and I loved each other deeply and that day we were united in our contempt for this photographer who was badgering us for cheesy smiles. My mother blamed our expressions on the sun.

I still have the newspaper cutting and can now see why it was such a great story. A modest young mother (don't mention the absent father) was suddenly thrust into the limelight by her devoted children who had secretly nominated her for the nearby town's annual beauty contest that led directly to regional heats, Miss UK and then the big one – Miss World watched by millions around the globe. This was still a time when beauty contests could transform the lives of a few working class women.

It was all Deborah's idea. She couldn't enter herself into the competition so she decided that we should do it instead. I thought it was a bad idea straight away but my mother could be very persuasive; backed up with bribes of Curly Wurly's and a box of Black Magic. My resolve was easily broken, besides I loved writing and I didn't mind filling out the form and explaining that Deborah was "amazing" and "not only the most beautiful Mum in the world but also the best."

How a newspaper editor believed an eight and five year old were able to find a suitable photograph, envelope and stamp to complete this secret deed, I have no idea. But by the time the photographer and reporter arrived at our ramshackle bungalow there was no going back. I obliged with the quote they wanted by elaborating on how we had come up with the idea after seeing the competition in the newspaper and had planned it as a big surprise for our mother. I didn't enjoy being in the spotlight and was relieved when they finally left and I could forget about the whole thing. That was until the following week when Deborah arrived home with a pile of Herald newspapers. To my horror, and her delight, the photograph of the three of us was on the front page of each and every one of them and, even worse, a copy of my smudgy, badly spelt entry form.

It wasn't that I had told fibs (except the rather small white lie that we had come up with the idea ourselves). The truth was I did at times think that my Mother was rather amazing and I certainly loved her a great deal. Even as a young child I could see that against all the odds she was a doing a good job in bringing us up on her own. Yet the newspaper cutting made me feel confused. Here was the evidence in grainy black and white that we didn't fit into our small coastal backwater. My mother was simply too young, too beautiful and wore flowers in her hair. While my friends' mums were adorned in striped blue aprons and home-made perms, mine hitched lifts, cooked brown rice and filled the house with books and incense rather than freshly baked fairy cakes. This was the final proof – wearing hot pants on the front page of the Herald – my cheeks burned from the embarrassment.

Of course, Deborah didn't win. Typically, she didn't read the small print: you could only enter if you were single. Well she was, but somehow I don't think eligibility expanded to single mothers even though they were a rare commodity back then. Even if she could have entered I suspect she had left it too late to compete with 18 year olds who didn't have to try to hide their stretch marks or the first signs of cellulite (not that we had ever heard of it thirty odd years ago). The newspaper photograph is a reminder that this was the last time my Mother seriously tried to use her beauty to improve our lives - sadly it was too late.

It could have been so different. Deborah won her first beauty competition at the age of 17 while still at school. Tall, with thick blond hair, strong dark features and a pale skin she not only stood out but had an edge of vulnerability that was fashionable in the 1960s. In her case it wasn't an act.

She won a contract with a top modelling agency that cut her hair and fitted her out with designer clothes. The newspaper cuttings of the time show her demurely staring out of the page with a severe bob, tight fitting black shift dress and strappy stilettos. Yet even as she sat there in the studio I was developing from a tiny cell that kept on dividing despite all attempts by my mother to ignore it.

Deborah was naïve and unlucky. First boyfriend. First sexual experience. First big life event. Pregnant at only 17 she was almost a child herself. As I started to press against her taut stomach she tried to ignore me by first immersing herself in her short lived modelling career and then the arrangements for a perfect wedding in an imperfect situation. This was no shotgun marriage. My grandparents told her she was too young to get married – she had her whole life in front of her and they would help bring up the baby. Why compound a single error with a multitude of problems. My mother ignored them. It was still the '60s and marriage and motherhood were deeply ingrained and Deborah wanted to buy into it fully.

And now another photograph. One that again reveals almost too much but at the same time nothing. It is a picture of a family wedding taken nearly a decade earlier on another glorious summer's day. My parents pose with their new in-laws against the flint backdrop of an ancient church stone wall in Sussex.

If you peer at the print you would think that perhaps my grandmother looks rather too stern for such a happy occasion while my grandfather just a little too sad. It is one of the few photographs I have of my father's parents and I have no idea of their names let alone assigning private thoughts to them. As for my father he is just a boy and, although he is grinning at the photographer, he looks completely out of his depth. He must be wondering how, at just 18, he has ended up at his own church wedding with a child on the way.

But again the only person who really demands your attention is Deborah. Newly wed she hides her bump of four months in an Audrey Hepburn style dress imported from a top Paris fashion house and paid for by her fledgling modelling career. She shimmers in the heat and smooth satin lines: the ivory white offset against the blood red stain of the roses she clutches in her hands and her single gold band. Deborah stands tall and looks straight into the camera with her dazzling smile. She ignores the bad omens collecting in the wings. This is her day.

Learning Another Language
by Joe Sheerin

Before I became an exile myself, I had a romantic notion that immigrants were a homogeneous group. After all we were in the same boat, strangers in a strange land, and I believed that the glue of shared insecurities would hold us together. That belief was tested early on.

When I arrived in England, I roomed in a Polish house near Archway station in London. As these Poles were the first 'foreigners' I had ever seen, much less spoken to, having come from a remote and mountainous part of County Leitrim in Western Ireland, I remember them very clearly. One always remembers first times; first lover, first night in hospital, first sight of Trafalgar Square; the second experiences are never quite as memorable.

Three Poles lived there, balanced by three of us Irish. The owner, Yann, was podgy and pale with thinning fairish hair. He had a gold tooth and was a pastry cook. His lady friend was called Ewa. She didn't really live there but was in and out of the place. She was Polish or Czech and she seemed quite old to me at the time. Looking back now she must have only been in her thirties, but time hadn't been kind to her. Anyway the young are remarkably bad judges of age. She worked in the kitchen of a Polish café in Junction Road. I often saw her on the way back. She always carried a small bag of leftovers. It was probably a perk of the job. Years later when I saw a photo of Mother Theresa I was reminded somewhat of Ewa: the same triangular face and the same dropping eyelids.

Anton Kowal (Tony) was in his twenties and had a big resentful face. His lower jaw sagged as if he had the weight of an anvil hanging from it and it was an effort to speak. Jashu was a dapper and taciturn man, aged somewhere between twenty and fifty. He kept himself fiercely to himself. Generally the Poles and we Irish rubbed together quite amicably. Blanche du Bois's swingeing put-down, 'The Poles are like the Irish only not as sophisticated,' wasn't true in this case. The Poles in this instance dressed well and took a pride in their general appearance. We, on the other hand, were severely challenged sartorially.

Of the two groups the Poles were more tragic than we were. They had been plucked untimely from their familiar lives by a terrible war, some of them having barely reached teenage, put into labour camps and were finally washed up on England's shore as part of the vast post-war flotsam. They were then marooned in England never being able to return to their now communist homeland. They conversed in Polish all the time speaking across us in the kitchen as if we weren't there or shouting up the stairs. They often looked melancholy. They sometimes drank vodka. They often played poker. They never sang. We, on the other hand, had come to England voluntarily and we could go back if we wanted to. We were noisy, energetic to the point of arrogance, and we sang.

I got to love the sound of their words and the rhythm of their language. After a bit I worked out that 'dzien dobry' meant hello or good day, or something. So I started using it. They were amused at first and replied in kind. Kowal was the only one who seemed to resent it and he would say, "How she cutting?" using the Irish idiom. I took to replying "Dobrze", which I reckoned meant okay, or something like that. It didn't please him. One evening when were both alone in the kitchen he looked at me and asked quite abruptly, "You want to speak Polish?" I did.

"You can speak a bit. Now, next you just learn, 'How are you'? And the answer, 'I am good'. O.K?". And so he taught me quite patiently but magisterially, the anvil on his jaw moving deliberately and slowly, "Te jestish pisda" (How are you) and "Tak. Jestem pisda" (I'm good, thanks). We did that language drill several times until I had it like a parrot.

Our social lives were limited to the weekends. Fridays and Saturdays we, Irish, went to Irish pubs and Irish dancehalls. The Poles either went to the dogs in Harringay or went to a Polish club down Tottenham Court Road. On Sundays we went to mass - the Poles went to a Polish mass in St Joseph's in Highgate. On Sunday nights we all went to the cinema, the Odeon in Junction Road. There was always an immense queue because the programmes changed on Sundays. There was generally a B film and everybody smoked. We didn't go together. The Irish went in one group; the Poles in another. Afterwards though we met up in the shared kitchen to discuss the film. It was the only time we really met up as a group. The Irish drank tea. The Poles drank coffee. The Sunday night after my language lesson, Kowal made an announcement.

"Joey speak Polish now. He know to say 'How are you' and ' I'm O.K thanks you'. Watch!"

They watched.

Tony: "Te jestish pisda."

Me: "Tak. Jestem pisda."

Jashu seemed amused by my language skills. He smiled, then laughed, the sound coming down his nose in a rivulet of little snorts. "You speak that good, Joey. You speak Polish really, like Pole. Kowal is good school-teacher." And he punched Tony lightly on the shoulder as he left. Mother Teresa looked surprised, mumbled something and made herself scarce.

As I was about to go to my shared room, Jann motioned me to wait.

"Kowal teach you wrong things." He sat on a chair facing me, his fingers interlocked, and he circled the thumb of his right hand on the palm of his left.

"You mussent use that word, 'pisda'. It not very nice. It's very baht word."

"What does it mean?" I thought I knew all the bad words.

"It mean," and he looked at his stubby white pastry-cook fingers. "It is...", examining his nails again, "how you say...? The spot where lady make pee-pee from."

I was shocked, not by the word which I knew, but by the nakedness of his description.

"Kowal is ignorant," he assured me. "He come from the border. More Rashin than Polish."

I felt angry and betrayed. A few days later I confronted Kowal. He wasn't in the least apologetic. In fact he was on the offensive.

"Look, Paddy, you speak your language. Let Poles speak Polish language." Referring to me as 'Paddy' had re-filed me inside the correct sub-group of immigrants. When my resentment subsided and I was able to think about it I began to see Tony's point of view. He was just protecting his identity. That identity was important to him and he didn't want any undeserving intruder muscling into his private world.

I was really no different. If any of the English people in the Gestetner's factory where I then worked (not that any of them ever would as they were hugely uninterested in Ireland and all things Irish), if they had asked me to talk about stooking corn or putting an edge on a scythe, or footing turf, I wouldn't have told them a thing. These were my secrets, were part of my identity. I wasn't minded to dilute them or share them with strangers. We exiles or immigrants or emigrants, whatever you might call us, are jealous of our pasts. It's the only unique and valuable thing we have. Our past is a warm blanket to sleep under, and in times of stress we hug it to us. Occasionally we hide under it and exclude decent, well-meaning people, who simply want to make contact.

Just to annoy Tony I didn't give up. I got a Teach Yourself Polish book and even thought of taking it at O' level, although I never got round to it.

A few weeks ago I was in Sainsbury's and there was this elderly bloke mopping the floor in slow motion. He was Polish and had recently arrived in England. We chatted a bit and I was surprised at how much Polish I had remembered. He was equally surprised.

No. I didn't use the P word.

November 1963
by Dee Hesling

I could tell something very dark had happened – the air was heaving with apprehension as assembly never happened at 8 am. Sister Pogham stood laden with worry and sadness as she began the Our Father. We shifted nervously each and everyone aware of some impending disaster.

"Our dear bother was gunned down in Dallas Texas by a murderous madman."

Who is she talking about, I wondered. I felt worried for everyone at home. Gradually the story unfolded as she told us JFK had been killed. He was a bit of a folk hero as he had been on a visit claiming our relations were his forefathers – we went to Mass instead of English first period. Poor Jackie and the two little orphans – how would they survive this mowing down of the central figure in their lives?

We were all mourning but none of us quite knew why. I wanted to go home.

My Timeline
by Julian Harvey

1969 Man on the Moon
Watching it on the box, then running outside to look at the moon.
1974 Spoons
I watched Uri Geller bend a spoon on TV. I thought he's got some weak metal spoon there.
1976 Hot Summer
Running into the sea with ladybirds all over me. Lots of people thought they were getting bitten by them. I now know this was their legs.
1977 Royal Jubilee
Listening to the Sex Pistols singing 'God Save the Queen'. They summed up how I felt about the Royals
1980 Reagan Elected
This now makes me think of a line in the Like Flint films. "An Actor as President".
1981 The Wedding
Standing on a stolen milk bottle crate, I was taller than everyone. Charles and Diana looked over, I could almost hear them saying look at that tall man.
1987 Bowie on Stage
People cheering, expectations high, waiting for an eternity, then suddenly he appears.

Out of Israel
by Julie Haywood

I was there when my partner went to buy brown tape from the supermarket to seal up the windows of our apartment because Saddam Hussein had said Iraq was going to attack Israel with mustard gas bombs.

I was there when my daughter was two weeks old and the Government of Israel were issuing sealed cots for babies and gas masks for adults.

I wasn't there when the Gulf War began as I'd decided to fly back to England – it wasn't a hard decision to make.

I was there when the war was declared over – I couldn't wait to go back again to the land my child was born in.

We stayed in Israel until she was two.

I was there when she spoke her first words and they were in Hebrew.

I wasn't there when she was three – by then we'd moved back to England.

Alive Again
by Michelle Brown

I remember sitting in my little council flat with man after man, faceless, nameless now, so desperate not to be alone. Serving white rum to gangsters, yardies and elderly domino-playing Jamaicans, high as a kite all the time, retching over a toilet bowl, heaving. Being so thin and unwashed, bruises and track marks covering my arms, feet and later my inner thighs. Prescription methadone with its sickly sweet taste, so sugary that unwary flies often gorged on it and died in the sticky grave.

And I remember a kind, tanned face with glasses, the man I met by a quirk of fate, who made me feel alive when I was almost dead.

What a Wonderful World

A Mad Ride
byJenny Corbin

Mad is a controversial word. Mad is bad in many people's eyes. Would it be better to say I lost the plot? I lost my marbles? A nervous breakdown? … or simply that I was working on my emotional intelligence and was a 'work in progress'?

Suffering and 'madness' often go hand in hand – but never let it be forgotten that any experience which enables development of the hereto hidden creative self can only be a good – no – a great thing.

So thank you Madness. My journey with you has been one of the most difficult of my life, but also one of great personal growth and a wealth of cathartic creative experiences.

It's a white knuckle roller coaster of the mind, your wits strapped securely to the imagination.

The ascent, a bumpy ride, provides your brave face with travel packs of adrenaline (and maybe a valium or two) which feed into the calm yet amazing beauty of the view at its highest point.

A plummet – to madness?

Expected yet unexpected, so fast it removes your breath through a siphon attached not only to your lungs, or your brain, but to every living cell.

A cocktail of emotions, rendering rational thought impossible.

Crisis over.

You plan, to the best of your ability, the rest of your journey, remaining mindful of the approaching highs and lows with restored rationality.

You hope.

Singing for our Lives
by Pat Bowen

If you can walk you can dance; if you can talk you can sing.
(African Proverb)

Have you ever been told not to sing? That you are tone deaf, that you can't join the choir...? These are mild versions of the silencing voices I heard as a child in the 1950s. The only place I could sing freely was in church where it would have been considered un-Christian to prevent me joining in with the hymns. My mother wasn't allowed to sing either except in church, and she once told me that her mother could never 'raise her voice in song' even there.

I didn't think much about singing as I grew up in the 60s and moved into life, relationships and parenting; never questioned why I was so often attracted to musicians – singers even. In 1986 I was shaken about by major life changes from which I 'woke' to discover that I had no idea what I enjoyed doing. For a single mother on a low income there weren't many options so when I saw a poster for a benefit event for Nicaragua at a nearby church hall on a night when I could get a baby-sitter, I went. There was circle dancing, sometimes to robust folk tunes with steps that leapt and spun, sometimes to more contemplative music with simple, quiet movements. Poems and talk about Nicaragua followed and then we learned "Singing for our Lives" by American feminist song-writer Holly Near:

We are a gentle angry people
And we are singing for our lives...
We are young and old together
And we are singing for our lives...

We continued substituting all the pairs of opposites anyone could think of: men and women, black and white, gay and straight. We danced as we sang – in a circle, hands on each other's shoulders enacting one of humanity's oldest symbols of connection and community.

I'd found something I enjoyed and began to look for more. There was a Voice Workshop at Brighton Natural Health Centre. First we listened to tapes of singers from other cultures and were startled to realise that we couldn't even tell whether they were male or female, let alone make sense of the tunes and harmonies. It became clear that there are more ways of using our vocal chords than any one culture comprehends.

Then we were led on a visualisation exercise. The room was light, the atmosphere one of gentle, trusting focus, and our guide skilful. I also must have been ripe for what happened next. Recounting it, I fear that

[88]

it sounds like a cliché but to me then it was new. We each took a foetal position on the floor with our eyes closed. We had to imagine ourselves alone and held deep in the earth. In this place we were invited to start to make sounds, still taking no notice at all of anyone else. As we made the sounds, we were encouraged to feel life come into our limbs and as it came, to feel the connection with the earth itself and the earth energies all around our still-curled-up bodies. After a while our limbs began to move until our feet connected with the floor and we felt the earth's support beneath them. All the time we were making whatever sounds emerged.

Suddenly there came awareness of another source of energy – the sun. Still with our eyes closed, we responded to this new source of power – we could move and stretch. My voice began to express a new-found joy – and shock of all shocks – I heard it sound beautiful. I had never for one second of my existence dreamed that I would hear a beautiful voice coming out of my body. Gradually we related to other people by making sounds together, and then to open our eyes and come back to ordinary space. I was in tears and trembling.

Wouldn't it be a good story if I could say "from that day, I was able to sing in tune and with a glorious voice"? Sadly, I can't say that. But it started me singing and what fun I've had. I've done a cappella harmonies with Brighton's wonderful Acabellas, now in their 19th year. I've sung Tagore songs and Indian ragas accompanied by crickets and fireflies beneath balmy Bengali skies. I've taken part in Klezfest and sung Niggunim and Yiddish songs in the synagogue. I've raised my voice with the Hove U3A singing English folk tunes, show songs, spirituals and funny rounds. I've organised evenings with friends putting subtitles on the DVD so we can sing-along to musicals with much laughter and raucousness. On occasion I've found deep relief from sadness by howling until fury and grief become a crooning lament. Once or twice I've even managed to sing a (simple) song to someone else without changing key midway.

There have been unforeseen consequences too. The Acabellas, the first choir with which I performed and where I sang happily for many years, is a women's collective – there's no leader and all members have equal power. There I learned the joys (and frustrations) of working co-operatively with people committed to mutual support and respectful ways of resolving difficulties. Such thoughtful, non-violent communication practices were a revelation and have stayed with me. They are a vital part of what makes the Acabellas radical, creative and fun.

Then there's the matter of singing with teachers from different cultures – first, Rajeswar Bhattacharya from Kolkata in West Bengal.

I've not been able to learn Bengali, but Rajeswar is particular about pronunciation and makes sure that we understand the words of the Rabindranath Tagore songs he teaches. And what words! Full of rhymes, assonance and rich, onomatopaeic sounds and rhythms, in lyrics and melodies that celebrate Life: flowers, smells, weather, seasons, rivers, Bengal itself and the connections between people, place, music – everything. My introduction to the beauty and subtleties in the sounds and meanings of these songs linked with an interest in the history and cultures of India and developed a sense of connection with the people there. I also have vivid memories of the surprise and delight in the faces of people in West Bengal (especially in rural areas and small towns) when they met a group of 'Britishers' who had come to learn their music. It felt good to be demonstrating respect and admiration for another culture, especially one where there has been a history of Western arrogance.

Of course I will never understand the fullness of Indian music – it's said that it takes many lifetimes to learn when you're born into it – and I can't even hear some of the subtleties of raga variations let alone sing them.

My latest vocal adventure is with the Brighton and Hove Yiddish choir led by Jewish music specialist Polina Shepherd who was born in the east of the former Soviet Union. I've found a way to stay in my home town and visit another ancient and diverse culture – I think I'll promote such singing as low-carbon-emission travel! The music ranges in mood from profound melancholy to mischievous humour, from trance-like meditation to ecstatic celebration, and singing it with other people creates a channel for expressing and sharing those states and emotions.

So learning to sing has been a healing journey that started deep inside me with the breaking of a silence at least three generations long. From there it has drawn me into connection with people from my own and other cultures – a connection made palpable by the sound of our voices in melody and harmony together. It feels like visiting other countries and being invited to share in feasts. I bet the same could be said of learning to dance – but that would be another story.

Nature as Therapy
by Richard Ince

When I am unhappy, sorrowful, stressed, a walk with nature restores me. Woods and downs, meadows and cornfields, heathland and lakes. The everchanging flowers from the snowdrops of winter, the spring anemones and bluebells, the agrimony and vipers bugloss of summer. Trees with their bare beseeching branches of winter to the autumn foliage that from afar look like huge tapestries. Animals, birds, insects. Is there anything more beautiful than the brilliant blue dragonfly darting and hovering in the sun? Or the velvet wings of the peacock butterfly, a glimpse of the red-brown fox on the field edge, or the kestrel high overhead?

The weather affects what you see. Have you ever looked closely at a snowflake before it melts? A cut diamond. A birch tree in the morning sunlight after a severe frost. The dewdrops on a spider's web. The magic of a full moon, especially away from city lights?

And what of your other senses? Touch the thistledown, soft as fuzz on a baby's head. Run your fingers through the tall grasses in the meadow – sensuous.

Smell the pungent wild garlic, the cow-parsley, the soporific scent of drying hay. See how the wind-driven cloud casts a shadow which races down the valley, and grasses ripple like the sea, on the hillside. Hear the raucous rooks, the hum of the bees, the sheep and cattle. Listen to the wind sighing spookily through the pines. And sometimes just listen to the silence.

Nature is also terrible. Creatures that we love kill and are killed, but there is one huge difference compared to mankind. There is no cruelty, no malice. They kill to eat – nothing more. Man is also part of Nature. Look at a local map. Tinker's Lane, Limekiln Wood, Poverty Bottom, Sandpit Wood, Beggar's Croft. Man worked and suffered. History is all around us.

Nature is in Brighton. That roadside tree is not an obstacle – it is beauty in its own right. Sit in the Pavilion Gardens, visit St Anne's Well Gardens, go to Stanmer Park. On the seafront the starlings give a free show every evening, weaving their amazing patterns across the sky. On rare occasions when out walking, I have a feeling of intense joy. I don't know where it comes from. It is gone in a second. Perhaps it is the exaltation that religious mystics described. I don't know – but for me it is heaven before death.

I wrote this in summer 2005 for the magazine of Brighton Unemployed Centre. Since then the Centre have organised monthly walks of between eight and ten miles, sometimes across the Downs, sometimes along the cliff tops, sometimes through the Weald. These have introduced people to the beauty and history of the countryside around Brighton.

In 2007 some of us went on a training course organised by Brighton and Hove Council to become Healthwalks leaders. Healthwalks are short, circular walks from one and a half to three and a half miles, either completely within the city or going out into the countryside. All starting points are accessible from city buses.

Following on from this, the Centre introduced short circular walks to Queen's Park, taking about one hour. These are ideal for all ages. The park is quiet and beautiful, a real neighbourhood resort: lots of mature trees, a wildlife area that is great for children, a scented garden, a huge pool full of water birds, grassy areas for children to play on, swings and slides, and a cafe.

We have combined two walks with picnics during the school summer holidays and have planned winter walks once a month. We want to show how much there is to enjoy in the city within walking distance. There is something for everyone, whether you want to get fitter, or you like nature or history, or just want good company and a chance to unwind.

Ewhurst 100 miles International Walk
by David Boxall

Left foot. Right foot. Lock those knees.
Marching sure wrecks memories.
One, two. Never three or four.
Strides are shortening, legs grow sore.
Left foot. Right foot. Keep this pace.
Forced smiles sure crease up the face.
Left foot. Right foot in a state.
"Eat bananas!" Far too late.
My whole schedule's gone to pot.
Legs are long gone, want to stop.
Should I eat or drink or what?
Pack it in. I just cannot.
Can I slow? No bloody fear.
The wife's shouting in my ear.
Do you want this? Do you want that?
She gives my bum a passing pat.
Am I getting paranoid?
Course, deep down I am overjoyed.
Sore and grumpy I hang on.
Bugger! All the water's gone.
All is negative, nothing's right.
On we go into the night.
Not a single soul gives in.
Paper cups show where we've been.
There's the wife. "How big's the gap.
How far to go?" "One more lap."
Deep inside I know it's more.
But hey, I know her hearing's poor.
It's pitch black but I hear a song.
I up the pace and swing along.
Even birds can tell the time.
Now I know the race is mine.
The final station's just ahead.
I try to smile but cry instead.
'Come on Dave'. I hear them shout.
Cast away is all self doubt.
Well, the job is all but done.
And they say race walking's fun.

Time To Say Goodbye

Time bomb
by Michelle Brown

The baby was my little secret. Early in the morning I would creep to the toilet and try my hardest to throw up quietly. Once after eating a full English breakfast in the greasy spoon around the corner, I didn't make it in time but festooned the floor and walls in glorious Technicolor. Sometimes I could almost forget, a coping mechanism I suppose, chain smoking away like I always had done. Other times I could not ignore the time bomb inside me. I would go to work in Soho, strutting about posing in my heels and black underwear, thin as a rail, and I would look down to where my belly was starting to curve and something hidden and delicious would slip inside me, a taste of things to come, a whisper that I was no longer alone.

I couldn't think my way round it. Sometimes it seemed like a lose-lose situation, and my mind would chase its tail round endless circles to nowhere. Other times, when I stopped thinking and just felt it, it was lovely; something not planned or wanted but primal and right.

Nearly four months passed by, and I still was no closer to a decision than the day I found out, when I had wandered, dazed, round Shepherd's Bush for hours, disbelieving and numb. I kept thinking that it couldn't be true, how could it, I was only 18, living in someone else's' house, with £22 a week JSA and £20 cash in hand from *Girls, Girls, Girls* to live on.

I had to decide. I had to do something. So I went off to Marie Stopes in Brixton. For days afterwards there was a dragging pain in my belly, like a fist clenching inside me, and I would see huge, bloody lumps of tissue in the toilet bowl, which I hysterically imagined might be bits of the baby. One night I awoke to find my breasts sticking to the bed sheets, covered in something wet and glutinous. When I realised my milk had come in, I cried and cried.

A Sailor's Last Voyage
by Maggs Radcliffe

I was there when fear and loneliness were my old friend's only remaining companions. Hungry Hungeford bravely navigated his last sea voyage on a vessel made of steel and springs; plastic sheets hugging an old dilapidated mattress his only foul weather gear.

A flotsam and jetsam of doctors and nurses bobbed in and out, to and fro, around the HMS Hungeford. But Hungry was prepared to exit stage left. His final words are to be my life epitaph: "it's hard by the yard, but a cinch by the inch…" The north wind blew cool as he gently closed his large brown orbs, at last breathing a farewell smile.

Decide
by Yvonne Luna

Career or baby? I'm sure I have a brilliant career ahead of me, so I can't let this get in the way. Besides, I've only known D a week. Of course I wasn't careful. You can't possibly be careful during your first week with someone, not if you're in wild, passionate LOVE. He would have thought I was frigid, or not really into him, not in LOVE.

Anyway, it turned out he must have wanted me to get pregnant. Years later, after we'd split up, he told me how upset he was about the abortion. He had a child already, you see. He knew about children. He wanted more. He knew it was a child I was killing. I didn't. I thought I was killing a party pooper that was going to stop me living a life. It wasn't a decision. I just did it. I didn't even think about it. You can make a mistake once. I had no regrets.

But I made a mistake twice. I call it a 'mistake' but I suppose really it was called a 'baby'. It might even have had more of a name than that one day. It might have been someone. And it would have had a brother or sister. This time it felt different. This time the decision felt like an incision cutting a child out of my life. The doctor made it harder too. He asked me if I wanted to think about it. He talked to me about how big it would be by now. But it's just a blob of cells, isn't it? And she's at University? he must have been thinking. No, he said, its got little feet and hands, a heart a head a face. Or maybe it was later I found that out. Surely I couldn't have done it if I'd known. Could I? The doctor reminded me of my age, mid 20s, a good time.

"But I don't know who the father is?!" It could be the guy who I only see if I happen to bump into him in the street. Or, if it's not his, it's my boyfriend's, and it would have been conceived on the night I visited him at 'La Colombiere', the mental hospital in Montpellier, the night I pushed the chair up against the door to jam the handle.

The doctor offered to do an examination. Why? It's only been just over a month. There won't be anything.

No, there'll be changes. And there were. He felt around inside me, said it all felt like it was progressing nice and normally. Go away and think about it.

I went home and straight away did my own examination. Oh my God. You can feel something. I'm pregnant. I lay there all night thinking I was going to have a baby. I could feel it inside me, growing. I filled with love for it.

By morning my head had taken over from my heart. I didn't know who the father was, and, either way it didn't look good: one didn't care, the other was mad. I myself was mad, stupid, depressed and selfish. What chance would it have? Hadn't my life been hard? Wouldn't its life be even harder? Be cruel to be kind. Make it all easy.

Don't ever ask me to make a decision about what to have off the menu, where to go on holiday, what to watch on TV. How are you ever supposed to trust yourself again?

one day you died
by Anthony Spiers

I have kept that memory in a buff
manila folder your name neatly handwritten
in biro on the front
just the way you would have done

along with candles
you might have thought were for you
a draught from somewhere worrying the pale yellow
flames in the electricity blackouts

and all those wings of course
not a blinding flurry of angels
bearing you aloft
no these were the wings of fruit flies

who love wine and I imagine
sober would have experienced little difficulty
towing your buoyant ghost into the sky
like tugboats

though in the laboratory they had to put up
with meals of yeasty custard
my eyes quizzing their dead wings
for mutations

I still find flies like those hungry
in the kitchen for the umber bananas
they bring no word of you
accounting at your desk in the endless white office

in the afterlife and gracing the calendar on the wall
Saint Joan or Mother Teresa
and you totting up somebody's sins in one column
kindnesses in another

Belonging
by Richard Ince

I'd walked up a steep hill, sweating, tired. The building was nondescript. I went into a grubby lobby. To the right were steep stairs with a roughly written notice: Brighton Unemployed Centre. I stood at the bottom to get my breath back.

I wasn't sure I wanted to join, but made myself climb up to the first landing. A small office led off.

A friendly voice said, "Can I help you?"

I felt more relaxed: "I'm interested in being a volunteer".

"Can you go up to the next floor and speak to Sheila? She'll be in the big room."

I tightened up. I don't like walking into rooms full of people I don't know.

However, I climbed up and opened the door. Unseen voices were singing quietly. A young child crawled around. He smelt of sick. There was a faint odour of cooking and coffee. People sat at tables drinking and talking. Across the room a young man was curled up on a sofa, fast asleep, hood over his head. People were painting glasses. Another older man was staring at a wall, lost in thought.he room was welcoming. Everyone seemed as though they belonged there. That's the word: "belonging". Someone pointed out Sheila to me and I introduced myself. She said she was in the middle of her Art Group and a tutor was about to talk about their new project. I was welcome to sit and listen. That was nice. I felt included. Afterwards Sheila gave me a Volunteer Application Form and information leaflet. I said I would join her writing group in the morning. I went downstairs feeling happy. The next morning I handed in my completed form at the office. A different person, but the same friendly response.

I had read the leaflet and the building felt more open to me now. There was a Welfare Rights room where you could get help from a trained worker. A computer room offering cheap courses and access to the Internet. The crèche was down that corridor, the kitchen over there. A room for courses and meetings. Somewhere downstairs was the laundry. The big room was busy.

I recognised a couple of faces from yesterday – Centre users, volunteers, paid workers. No one was labelled – just everyone working for the benefit of all. A smiling face approached and introduced itself as Charles.

I had a warm feeling of belonging.

A lot has changed since that day in February 2005 but two and a half years later I am still a volunteer at the Centre.

I started with a session on the reception desk and front office which I still do. This is interesting and at times very busy. You are the first person that visitors see, so you have to greet them and find out what they need. Perhaps they want to see a Welfare Rights advisor, or book a course or use the laundry or the computer room. The phone rings a lot and you have to answer the caller's questions if you can, or pass them on to a worker or take messages. You have to take in money from different sources and pay out expenses and balance the accounts at the end of the day. The Centre has very many different functions, and being on the desk is a great way to get to know them. Even more important, you begin to understand how much suffering there is in the community and in a little way you can to alleviate it. I think I am a more understanding, patient and helpful person since I have been working here.

I know how many committed people work in the Centre. The trustees are all former Centre users, the great majority of volunteers are also users. Eight out of nine of the paid workers were here when I started, and many of them for much longer, which speaks for itself.

I also help in the production of the Centre magazine, which is very satisfying. Everyone involved is a user or volunteer. Thanks to the Participation worker here, who knew I loved walking, I have had training to become a leader on Council Healthwalks. As a result of this we have started short walks from the Centre for adults and children which we hope will become popular. This is a good example of how people are encouraged to develop their skills for which I am very grateful.

So for me and many, many other people, 'belonging' is still the right word. The Centre is part of my life.

Life's A Carousel
by Judith Greenfield

I've suddenly realised that I've been here before.

I'm sitting here at the Centre eating a huge plate of sweet-smelling spicy dinner, chattering going on all around me and children, too wound up to sit still and eat, running about and playing with the toys.

I turn to my friend. He's been around quite a while maybe he will remember.

"Did this used to be a Singles Club?"

"Yes, I believe it did".

I'm right. Back in 1980, this building in Tilbury Place, which is now the home of the BUCFP, was the Carousel Club for single people who wanted to make new friends. I'd heard about it because the lady who ran it, I forget her name now, lived near me in Lancing. It was somewhere I could go on my own. I'm not very good in gangs of girls.

I remember being made very welcome. There was different sorts of dancing on different nights, a bar with snacks and a quiet lounge area. There was a real mix of people of all ages. I loved ballroom dancing and I remember having a regular partner who was a competition walker. Boy, did he take some keeping up with.

I know now that this is the building but it's much bigger in my memory. Where has all the space gone? It's a puzzle to me. Perhaps there's bits I haven't discovered yet.

Actually I met my husband here all those years ago. I was generally happy to arrive and leave on my own and just enjoy the friends I had come to know for the time I was there. I wasn't looking for anything more. But that's life.

Things turn up when you aren't searching for them. I did try to play it cool for a while but you know how it goes.

Twenty seven years later here I am back in Tilbury Place absolutely loving the writing course and the people I share it with. Sadly my husband passed away and I'm out and about on my own again doing things I enjoy. Who knows?

I Love This Class
by David Boxall

I love this class   though life is seldom easy here.
Weeks gallop past   they come from far and near.
Willows and oaks   fresh grass and moss.
Heaven meets earth   life's not veneer or gloss.

I love this class   the openness within each free.
Half empty then   oh dear, we're out of space.
We hear the tots   when singing starts
They keep us young   God bless their little hearts.

I love this class   and yet it's bedlam by midday
Now here it comes   "Let's all go out and play".
The sun pours in   we work I drive
Cause after all   It makes us feel alive.

I love this class   kitchen dishes start to clatter
It's silent now   but for muffled chatter.
Julie's in charge   it works that way.

All finished class   evaporated. Off they go.
Each to their home   where? I don't need to know.
It's only now   as minutes pass
I realise.   You know. I love this class.

This Much I Know
by Polly

As a child I remember that my sister used to wear red and blue gingham dresses and I always had the desire, the compulsion, to dress up in them.

When I started secondary school I had to suppress these kind of feelings. I was pushed into doing things I didn't want to do: more boyish pursuits. As a child I was always playing with my sisters rather than my brothers. I was depressed because I wasn't doing the things I felt happiest doing.

When I left school at 16 I was able to do things I wanted to do like buying my own clothes, although I still had to wear them secretly in my bedroom.

When I got married I was truly happy to marry the girl I loved. Again, I put my feelings on hold or suppressed them because I didn't want to upset her. But she knew. I told her that I had felt this way for years because I wanted to be honest.

From 13 onwards I knew something was wrong with me. As a boy I was feeling pains that shouldn't be felt by a boy. When my sister started her periods I had the same kind of pain. I kept it to myself because I thought I was barmy. I thought I was sick in the head. I kept it all shut up. When I was in my teens I used to lie back in my bed and wonder if I was a girl: if I would wake up one morning with boobs.

I'm sure my Mother knew because she'd found stuff in my bedroom, stuff that I was keeping secret and, of course, she'd know what I was like when I was a kid and how I'd dress up in my sisters' dresses.

There were times in my life when I knew I was in the wrong body. I felt torn apart. I'm sure it contributed to the nervous breakdown I had four years ago. Things were going wrong in my marriage, although I loved my family and still do. It's difficult for me to start a relationship because it would feel like committing treason to my family, even though I know we will never get back together again. I've always believed in miracles but I know this is one that won't happen.

The older I get the more determined I am to be the person I want to be – not how I am today. But I worry about dressing the way I want because I would hate to upset or offend anyone, especially people at the Centre that I like. I've confided in a counsellor and also in people at the Centre and they all tell me the same thing: if others are offended it is their problem, not mine. But it's still hard to go ahead with it. I'm in a whirlwind at the moment, not sure what to do.

But one thing's for certain, the Centre has opened my eyes and opened my heart.

The Authors

A.K.Andrew has pursued the arts throughout her life. She has performed as a singer, musician and tap-dancer. In London she worked in community arts and in San Francisco was a fetish-clothing designer. As a painter, her work has been exhibited in both the USA and UK.

Allison Clare says you can take the girl out of Whitehawk but you can't take Whitehawk out of the girl...somehow she still managed to get a Masters degree. Survived the Mill View experience. Now happily volunteering and using Holistic Therapy. Proudly unconventional and no longer a victim.

Anthony Spiers absurder buspassbody cleanshaver dunglooker earthyman fruithounder gowalkabouter hairyheadling imaginationist jazzmouther knucklewiggler londonbaby myopian noisyphobe ownteethkeeper poemer quirkperson rockpuddlian shortheightguy tinbanger upatcloudslooker verbalcook weedpeeper xychromosomeowner yafflelistener zoolist

Bernie O'Donnell was born in Birmingham to Irish Parents and brought up on a large 50's Macmillan Housing Boom Council Estate. "Never had it so good". To Brighton for free university education; "white heat of...(technological) revolution". Worked in London to help develop our computerised society; "no such thing as society".

Candida Ford

David Boxall born 1933 Newhaven. Early interests included painting, science fiction, athletics. Came second in European 100k walking championships aged 46. Competed in forty 100 mile races, winning eleven. Equalled world record of 133 miles in 24 hours. Started yoga in 1985. Since 1995 has written 4,000 short stories and poems.

Dee Hesling is a senior staff nurse and works in emergency care at the County Hospital. She loves travelling and recently spent a month in Thailand where she visited Bangkok hospital to share and compare clinical practice. She has worked in Africa, USA and Australia. She loves her job and loves Brighton.

Ged Duncan grew up in Brighton where he still often skulks. Otherwise he may be in a shed in Dorset where he campaigns for the appreciation of Oliver, rather than Thomas, Hardy. He writes and tells stories for children and adults.

Gordon Radcliffe was born in Holmfirth, Yorkshire. He studied his way through the ranks and fulfilled his professional career as pathologist. By inclination a sailor, he latterly washed ashore on the shingle of Brighton.

Jaelithe Casteel is 35 years old and proud of it! She has battled through a multitude of obstacles in her life and becomes very offended when asked to prove her age in pubs. Jaelithe is happy to accept commissions, especially in exotic locations.

Jenny Corbin is extremely grateful to BUCFP for the opportunity to explore her creative side which has been under lock and key for years! Painting and writing can be cathartic outlets for difficult emotions and the Centre has provided a safe space in which to do just that. So thank you!

Joe Sheerin was born in Co Leitrim Ireland in 1941 and came to England in the fifties. He has had lots of jobs, done some travelling and has recently retired, having spent the last twenty five years teaching English at a Sixth Form College.

Josephine

Josie Darling grew up wanting to be a magician's assistant or a deep sea diver. She still wishes to fulfil these aims before she ends up in an old people's home.

Judith Greenfield was born in Yorkshire in 1947 and journeyed south via Berkshire to Sussex. After a varied working life, two marriages and one son, she is enjoying her retirement, travelling extensively and acquiring lifelong friends on the way. She fills her time with writing, acting, comedy and performing with her band.

Julian Harvey is interested in photography, aircraft and classic cinematography. He took part in Salt and Vinegar to see where it would take his writing and to meet new people.

Julie Hayward works as a cleaner through choice, which surprises many people. She thinks cleaning's great. It gives her the flexibility and freedom to travel, so when her 16 year old daughter says 'Mum do we have to go away AGAIN', she can say 'yes, get your bags packed. We're off.'

Laila Raphael lives with her five year old child in Brighton. Of mixed race origin, she grew up with adoptive parents, travelled and lived abroad a lot. She feels that she belong to an international community rather than belonging to one particular place. She likes art, music, nature.

Maggs Radcliffe USA: Illinois mid west born and bred, navigating "the mid-life seas" with ink dipped paddles…wants her message in a bottle to wash ashore! Heads up! Part-time Brightonian transplant….

Malcolm Williams

Margaret

Michelle Brown lives on a converted bus with her partner. She is a party animal and raconteur who likes music, dancing, budgies, dogs, weight training and boxing. She's led a colourful life but has settled down (somewhat).

Pat Bowen has lived in Brighton since 1969, raised a family, cultivated allotments and worked as a teacher and a storyteller. Her explorations of Sussex on foot, bike and bus have resulted in a book – *20 Sussex Walks* published in 2007 by Snake River Press.

Polly

Richard Ince's job moved from Nottingham to Portsmouth In 1995. At his wife's request he decided to live in Brighton, which he never regretted despite the awful travelling. He retired in 2004 and not being a sit-at-home type, found his way to the Centre which also he has never regretted.

Richard Laidler

Rob Stride is a very old musician, passionate about music, comedy and art. A solo artist, he also plays in two bands *Spyderbaby* and *Dogs Will Be Dogs* (featured in myspace & CDBABY). His two sons Michael and Steven have their own band, *When Logic Dies*. Like his dog, Rob distrusts politicians.

Sandy Gee moved 20 years ago from her native northern illumination-proud Blackpool to southern pebbly, cultured, 'alternative' Brighton. An avid reader, she's only written letters/emails/diary entries and the odd academic essay before. She loved the chance to be tutored to write more richly and experimentally about her own life and experience.

Sanjay Kumar was delivered by his grandmother in his ancestral home in Calcutta. Born in a garden of pomegranates, mangoes and orchids next to the family temple dedicated to Vishnu, he has lived in Brighton since 2005 and works with The Prince's Trust. He is a trustee and fervent supporter of BUCFP.

Shelley is a loving, supportive woman and mother, who lived for six years in Jamaica, Australia and Thailand. She's passionate about astrology and holistic alternatives to living a healthy and happy life. Loves cooking, reading and writing and is currently studying at college, volunteering at BUFPC and preparing to launch her business.

Ty Galvin was born in Cork and through various circumstances came to England in his teens. Having worked all over Britain as an electrician and cable jointer on the electrification of the railway, he came to Brighton in 1970. He subsequently worked for two years on the renovation of the Palace Pier

Valérie de Schaller was born in Switzerland. At the age of nine and three-quarters she moved to England with her family. This has left a disturbing division between her life as a child and her challenges in adult life in England. She now lives contently with her cat on the outskirts of Hove.

Yvonne Luna is a lady from Hove who, despite travelling the world, always boomerangs back to Brighton. She is currently in love with Eugene Hutz of Gogol Bordello, lives in a world of her own, talks to herself, and has three pet seagulls.

Some of the people behind the scenes

Bridget Whelan Writer in Residence teaches creative writing in London and Brighton. A prize winning short story writer, she has been awarded an Arts Council bursary to complete her first novel.

Ellie Moulton Participation Worker is an enthusiastic knabber of potential volunteers. She has fallen deeply in love with a beach hut on the seafront and has never been known to sit down.

Lisa Marshall Fundraiser BC (before children) used to win *Mars* bar eating competitions and jump out of airplanes, but AD (*Anno Domesticus*) spends her days trying to get her daughter to tidy her room and dreams of stopping time.

Peter Sutcliffe Education Worker was born under a bad sign. If he didn't have bad luck he'd have no luck at all. Despite this, he is available for hire as a tap dancer: parties, weddings, bar mitzvahs, all occasions considered.

Naomi Foyle performance poet and creative writing tutor.